Own
Your Network

**Expert Networking
in Person and Online**

Nadia Bilchik

GREATER
impact
COMMUNICATION

This book is a work of non-fiction. Unless otherwise notes, the author and the publisher make no explicit guarantees as to the accuracy of the information contained in this book and in some cases, names of people and places have been altered to protect their privacy.

First published by Greater Impact Communication 07/15/2018

ISBN: 978-0-9885013-3-1

E-Reader ISBN: 978-0-9885013-4-8

Library of Congress Control Number: 2370000464170

Edited by Topflight Communication, Inc., www.topflightcommunication.com
Interior designed by Bryan K. Reed, www.bryankreed.com
Cover by: Conny Bolter, www.bolter.info

Printed in the United States of America

To Steve, Alexa, and Julia
My network at home that makes all the rest possible

ACKNOWLEDGMENTS

I want to thank my friend, mentor and colleague, Daphne Schechter, who saw the need for internal company networking within the Coca-Cola Company, and then worked with me to develop the networking for success program. Many of the ideas and concepts embodied in networking for success have become the inspiration for this book.

This book would not have happened without the skill and talent of Miriam Lacob Stix, who helped me translate every one of my seminars into readable sentences. Thank you for the hours spent researching every aspect of networking and for the late night calls and endless edits.

Thank you also to Suzanne Hanein, my dear friend, who helped me put together all the materials for my seminars when I first came to America. Without your knowledge, insight, and creative computer publishing skills, writing anything would still be a dream.

Special appreciation to the wonderful people I work with at the CNN, who demonstrate the benefits of mutually reciprocal networking on a daily basis.

Appreciation also to Cliff Carle, whose organizational skills and discipline have kept us all on track and turned a manuscript into a book.

Thank you to Dina Fuchs-Beresin and Michelle Watson for assisting me in updating my original book, *The Little Book of Big Networking Ideas*, and injecting energy and enthusiasm into the editing process. I truly appreciate the endless cups of coffee and conversation.

TABLE OF CONTENTS

INTRODUCTION

Whatever we have accomplished has been because other people have helped us.

—Walt Disney, Entrepreneur and Film Producer

There are people who have been blessed with an organic network developed over a lifetime, consisting of the people they grew up with and went to school with—family members, playground friends, teachers, and family acquaintances. But this is not always the case, particularly among young adults and people who are more mobile and adventurous. People move away from their original home for jobs to improve their lives, and sometimes because they feel they have no choice. In my case, we moved from Johannesburg, South Africa, when my husband was offered the opportunity to join an exciting real estate start-up.

Americans are an especially mobile group of people. For example, the U.S. Census Bureau reports that 35.9 million U.S. residents, or 11.7 percent of all Americans, moved between 2012 and 2013. And, Americans reportedly move an average of 11 times during their lives. Surveys have found that young adults have the highest moving rates, with the higher educated moving longer distances for work. Those with a bachelor's degree or higher are most likely to have moved 500 miles or more.

If you have moved for employment reasons, you are not alone. In most cases, job-specific relocation is a pursuit for the young. One major moving company's annual corporate relations survey found that 93 percent of all transferees were between the ages of 25 and 45. Among the most highly mobile are business executives, who tend to make long-distance moves, mostly for work-related reasons.

Most people migrate to better their circumstances and take advantage of new opportunities—as embodied in the idea of seeking "greener pastures." But moving—whether it is changing cities, or simply starting a new job across town—can also be a real challenge. It tears the individual away from a network of relatives and lifelong friends who provide valuable financial advice, healthcare, and many other types of support. Think of it like being a frequently repotted plant: mobility tends to disrupt social root systems. A mobile lifestyle presents individuals with the task of having to continually rebuild a network from the ground up.

My Personal Story

I faced exactly that task, rebuilding my entire network, when I moved from South Africa to Atlanta, Georgia with my family in 1997. We moved to take advantage of a once-in-a-lifetime opportunity to immigrate to the United States for the stability and wonderful opportunities this country offers. But, it was not without pain and loss. I was a prominent television anchor in my home country and owned a thriving business. I had a brilliant career and an extensive, organic network of people, many of whom I had known all of my life.

I lost a lot in making the move—a beautiful home, proximity to my parents, and a fabulous climate. Little did I know that one of the biggest losses of my move to the United States was the loss of my network, which extended back for generations. My grandfather came to South Africa from Russia in 1929. He founded a contract painting company called E. Bilchik and Co., and by the time I was born, Bilchik Wallpapers was a household name. I was therefore born into a network that included everyone I needed, from the family insurance broker to the family doctor.

In South Africa, when I started my own communications company, and I needed a loan for equipment, I had only to pick up the phone to my father's bank manager. Without so much as a signature, I had access to unlimited funds. When I left my car's parking brake off and it rolled into the neighbor's electricity pole, all I needed to do was call the family insurance broker, and my car was towed away and all the bodywork bills were paid. And, when I became a professional media and presentation skills coach, all I needed to do was mention it to a high school friend, who had recently been appointed editor of a Sunday newspaper, and the promotional editorials flowed. Such is the power of an "organic network"!

As a newcomer to Atlanta, I left all of that and more behind. I had the daunting task of building a completely new network from scratch. And now, every time I stand in front of a group of people at Turner Broadcasting or one of its subsidiaries, The Coca-Cola Company, Delta Technology, Accenture, or Bellsouth, I remind each and every person that I would not be there if it was not for my ability to network.

It is not a process that has happened overnight. Nor was it accomplished in some magical and mysterious way. It was achieved through hard work and the application of many common sense networking strategies. Rebuilding my network with the principles and steps you are about to read worked very well for me, and because of that, networking has become my passion.

The purpose of this book is to demonstrate that developing the highly effective networking skills, which I call "expert networking," is neither mysterious nor magical. Rather, it involves powerful, yet easy-to-learn, strategies and approaches to relationships that you can make a part of your own skill set.

This book will take you step-by-step through the process of *expert networking*, and give you the opportunity to practice many of the strategies I share with you along the way.

As you work your way through the book you will:

- Understand the true nature of networking
- Analyze and overcome any of your own personal obstacles to networking
- Develop a new paradigm of networking that can be transformational
- Learn to recognize potentially fruitful relationships
- Practice transforming new interpersonal encounters from a connection to a conversation to a collaboration
- Find and develop targeted networking opportunities
- Become skilled at follow-up
- Become a networking "go to" person—a truly powerful position to be in

How to Use This Book

In this book, I'm not just going to lecture to you. I'm going to invite you to:

1. Actively create your own tools for success
1. Reflect on your own conscious and subconscious behavior
1. Develop and expand your network

This will all be accomplished through self-reflection and diligently working on the series of exercises that are provided.

You can either read the book all the way through to get an overview, then come back and do the exercises, or you can do the exercises as you come to them.

Most of the exercises require some writing on your part. I provided space to write directly below each exercise, but you may prefer to write on a separate sheet of paper or in a journal. There is a section at the back of the book labeled "Notes," which you can use for answering the questions, or to jot down ideas that come to you. In many cases, you may need to reflect a little before responding to the exercises. The Notes pages are a convenient way to keep your brainstorming and exercise responses in one place.

You may find that your responses will change as you go further down the road of expanding your network. It may be helpful to make extra copies of the exercises so you can compare your earlier and later responses. However you do it, always keep in mind that the more diligently you participate in the exercises, the greater your results will be.

CHAPTER 1

What Is a Network?

We cannot live for ourselves alone. Our lives are connected by a thousand invisible threads, and along these sympathetic fibers, our actions run as causes and return to us as results.

— Herman Melville, Author

The path to success in many fields begins with clear definitions. It is all very well talking about the importance of networking for life and career success, but it is a useless conversation without a clear understanding of what it means to have a network.

Having a social network means having a group of people who are invested in you sufficiently enough to have a stake in your well-being and success—and vice versa. It is important to note here that members of your network can be your friends and relatives, but not necessarily. More likely, it is the connections you develop with people who are not close to you by virtue of blood ties or friendship that may carry the biggest rewards. Either way, what's essential to *expert networking* is that you find a way to make a *reciprocal* connection with someone, which will be to the advantage of *both* of you.

My relationship with Daphne Schechter is a good example of this kind of mutually beneficial relationship. I met Daphne through a friend. Daphne had created the Coca-Cola mentoring program during her tenure, and she brought me in to teach a program on intra-company networking. She has become a wonderful champion, mentor, and friend. Daphne recently left Coca-Cola to start her own company, and I have recommended her as a speaker and consultant to several of my clients. We have also worked together to create a wonderful program on "Greater Impact Presentations." Thus, the collaboration continues.

If you can visualize a telephone network, you will understand that networks are never unidirectional. *Expert networking* is never a one-way street. It is vital to keep in mind that you have become part of a two-way, or even multidirectional process in which what you bring to the table becomes a vital element.

As networking guru Susan Roane says, "networking is a reciprocal process based on the exchange of ideas, information and knowledge, where resources are shared and acknowledged."

In the truest sense of the word, it means having a group of people whom you invest in, care about, nurture, and have at the forefront of your mind. These are people who will go the extra mile, and who want to see you succeed—and always vice-versa! A true member of your network will take your resume to the head of marketing, rather than just directing you to a job search website. But people take that step because they are certain *you* would make a similar trip on their behalf.

Both of you are invested in a long-term connection. One in which you have made a commitment to use your connections to help each other throughout your lives and careers. This relationship will allow you to give of yourself in such a way that the person you are networking with feels sufficiently invested in your well-being—so much so that they will trustingly and automatically try to move you forward in an effort to see you succeed. It could be for your career, or it could be for your personal life. Either way, that's what a network truly is.

The idea of "networking" is not new. As social scientist Bonnie Nardi points out, the term *networking*, as in "cultivating useful others," has been in use since at least 1940. What is new, she emphasizes, and I agree totally, is "the intensity and absolute necessity of networking for practically everyone." Networking takes *effort*. Nardi and her colleagues have even dubbed it "netWORK" in recognition that successful people work hard at establishing and managing their personal and professional relationships.

Advantages of Networking

Is netWORKing worth the effort?

Definitely.

Skillful and generous networking has proven to be vital for career success. The social resources people develop over time are known in the social sciences as "social capital." Researchers have found very strong links between social capital and career success, mainly because it facilitates access to social resources. These are, for example, access to hard-to-obtain information, business resources, and career sponsorship.

Indeed, studies of successful managers have found that they spend 70 percent more time networking and 10 percent more time communicating with the people they manage or encounter in the course of their work than their less successful counterparts.

Successful managers network 70% more than less successful managers.

Networking is also a skill that helps you overcome a wide range of barriers, be they social or physical. As networking expert Rick Frishman points out, "In today's world, where the best people are protected by electronic fences and are impossible to reach, good networkers can get through and do so in a way that can get their targets to actually listen and act."

The ability to develop and maintain a personal social network is also an extremely adaptive response to the changing nature of the workplace where old and set hierarchies and forms of organization are rapidly becoming obsolete. A group of anthropologists who studied personal social networks in the workplace concluded that they have become a key social structure for enabling work. Frishman says this is because networking is the "main form of social organization in the workplace as a dazzling new battery of communication technologies enables workers to connect to diverse, far-flung social networks."

Nardi notes that, because workers are no longer supported and nurtured by an institutionalized group structure, they are increasingly thrown back on their own individual resources. Instead of being able to rely on various forms of teams and communities, access to labor and information comes through workers' own social networks—structures which they must carefully propagate and cultivate themselves.

In this kind of environment, individuals have much better control of their working lives if they become successful at creating and maintaining personal social networks. Unfortunately, it's not the kind of work you can put on a timesheet. Rather, networking is a kind of "invisible work" not accounted for in workflow diagrams or performance evaluations. But, smart workers know they have to take it on so they can do their jobs effectively and make the kind of progress they know they deserve.

Multiple Payoffs of Networking

If this all sounds very daunting, let me assure you that all your hard work will have a payoff in ways far beyond career advancement. Social scientists like Nan Lin of Duke University have found that access to and use of the social resources that networks offer can lead to better socioeconomic status. It comes in terms of occupational status, more authority, a better position in certain industries, and, of course, the size of your paycheck.

Why do you reap these benefits? Because you will have better and more timely access to information, and better access to financial and material resources, as well as higher visibility.

There is a further impetus for people to move beyond their own limited social circle. People who have ties outside of their social clique often have increased access to unique information and resources. Studies have shown that individuals who can access the information from the members of their social network, who are not close friends and relatives, are likely to have better information about job openings, and better access to contacts in other social groups. Similarly, an Academy of Management Journal study (2001) showed that individuals with multiple mentors reap greater career benefits than those having only one mentor.

Social networks are also good for our general well-being. Numerous studies have shown that having social support decreases the heart-racing, blood pressure-boosting responses that human and other social animals have to stress. Researchers at Ohio State University and Carnegie

Mellon University have shown that people who report strong social supports have more robust immune systems and are less likely to succumb to infectious diseases.

Having social support boosts your immune system.

Thomas Rutledge and his colleagues, who conducted research in San Diego, found that women with more social contacts and who saw their contacts more often had lower blood glucose levels, lower blood pressure, and lower rates of smoking. Women with larger social networks also showed fewer signs of artery blockage during the four-year study. Not surprisingly, another study found that older men who have few personal relationships may have increased risk of heart disease.

Bonnie Erickson, a professor of sociology at The University of Toronto, reviewed research on people's social networks in several countries. She found that knowing many kinds of people in many social contexts improves one's chance of getting a good job, developing a range of cultural interests, feeling in control of one's life, and feeling healthy. In a study of participants in a Toronto social movement, she found that people with diversified general networks experienced less depression and were healthier.

Stephens's story: *Some years ago I was an executive at a magazine company. A young man called to ask if he could network with me and, as I almost always do, I told him I'd be happy to see him. We talked for about an hour or so, he sent the obligatory thank you note, and that was that.*

About six months later I received another note from him, inviting me to a party to celebrate his new job. I went and met an interesting young woman with dark, curly hair and blue eyes, with whom I spent most of the night talking. This same guy belonged to a group that rented a house in Westhampton over the summer, and he invited me to another party to meet the members of the group, with the possibility of joining them. I went, and that same young woman—the one with the curls and the blue eyes—was there. We talked more, saw each other all summer, and, about a year later, were married.

There's still more. That new job the original networker landed was as an executive at a large communications company. He later invited me to join the company, which I did. So, out of the simple act of agreeing to be a networking source, I ended up with a place for the summer, my wife, and a new job.

As demonstrated by Stephen's story, these benefits can extend well beyond your working life. Researchers recently conducted a longitudinal study of retirees, and found that the most powerful predictor of life satisfaction right after retirement was the size of a person's social support network.

Life satisfaction after retirement is directly related to the size of your social support.

The study of social networks and the process of building "social capital" has become a respected field of academic study. Lin has quite systematically analyzed the advantages of building social networks, and developed a theory of social resources. In her definition of social capital, she makes it clear that building a network is a form of investment. She goes on to say that reciprocation is a vital part of the equation, because social capital is a form of "public good" that will fall apart if the individual members of the network become free riders. Lin defines social capital as "investment in social relations by individuals through which they gain access to embedded resources to enhance expected returns of instrumental or expressive actions."

Lin proposes several explanations as to why social networks are advantageous. For one, she notes, the flow of information is facilitated.

"Social ties can provide an individual with useful information about opportunities and choices otherwise not available. Likewise, these ties may alert an organization and its agents about the availability and interest of an otherwise unrecognized individual."

This information also makes it easier for organizations to recruit more skilled and better-qualified workers, and for employees to find organizations that can use their "capital" and provide appropriate rewards. Social ties also help establish the credentials of an individual, and they reinforce an individual's sense of identity and recognition. Lin says

Being assured and recognized of one's worthiness as an individual and a member of a social group sharing similar interests and resources not only provides emotional support, but also public acknowledgment of one's claim to certain resources. These reinforcements are essential for the maintenance of mental health and the entitlement to resources.

Your network is, or soon will be, a group of people who care about you and who have a stake in your progress and success. Likewise, you will have a stake in theirs. The advantages are many for all aspects of your life, including your career, social life, and your general sense of well-being.

CHAPTER 2

Obstacles to Creating a Network

Commit yourself to a dream. Nobody who tries to do something great, but fails, is a total failure. Why? Because he can always rest assured that he succeeded in life's most important battle. He defeated the fear of trying.

—Rev. Robert H. Schuller, Author and Pastor

Most individuals are well aware that career and personal success depends, in almost equal amounts, on *whom* you know, as well as *what* you know. Or, as world-renowned management expert, Tom Peters, says, "It is what you know about who you know." But that does not stop most people from freezing and shutting down when faced with a networking opportunity, be it a company gathering or a town picnic.

As a savvy socializer, Susan Roane asks, "If working a room is so much fun and so profitable, why do our hearts thump, our palms sweat, and our eyes glaze over when we think about it?" If this describes you, it is essential to delve deeply into what is stopping you. Ask yourself:

- What prevents me from investing in the people around me?
- What prevents me from becoming the kind of person who invests in other individuals in such a way that they automatically want to reciprocate?

It's true that some people avoid networking because they have been burned in some way by people who have taken advantage of them. But more people have subconscious obstacles blocking them from networking (or developing relationships) because of their negative perception of what networking is. In my networking skills classes, which I have taught throughout the world, individuals express many of the same concerns and fears.

What are these fears?

Many people tell me they are afraid of making a fool of themselves. Others are afraid of speaking to strangers and being perceived as pushy. Most people fear rejection, lack confidence, can't spare the time, or are unsure of how to identify good environments in which to network. Yes, the obstacles can be expressed in all kinds of elaborate ways, but they all come down to *fear*. Fear is the prime factor, and "time" is the excuse.

Exercise: *Identifying Your Conscious and Subconscious Obstacles to Networking*

At this time, you need to be totally honest with yourself. Try to identify the factors that hold you back from these three crucial networking activities.

WHAT STOPS YOU FROM...?

1) Initiating a conversation with a stranger

_____

_____

2) Developing deeper and more reciprocal relationships with your co-workers and friends

_____

_____

3) Reaching out to potential mentors, employers and resources

---

Do words like "uncertainty" and "fear" appear in your responses? These are common concerns, and that should be your first realization. Everybody experiences uncertainty and fear when faced with the unknown. In this case, it could be a person, or a group of people you may not know at all, but whom you need to get to know and hopefully develop a relationship with. If this is a frightening prospect, it may be helpful to realize that fear of rejection is very deep-seated. In fact, a study of the brains of individuals who were subjected to rejecting situations revealed that this experience activated the same part of the brain that is involved in physical pain. The scientists who reported this research theorized that this link developed because social relationships are so important to an individual's survival.

Therefore, if your goal is to approach a group of strangers without feeling the fear of rejection, then you are not being realistic. Rather, it is important to recognize that you are experiencing a normal response to a personally challenging situation. It may also help to remember the words of Senator John McCain,

"Courage is not the absence of fear; it is taking action despite the fear."

Changing the Paradigm

How many times have you come home from a business or social event with a pocket full of business cards and no intention of ever calling one of them? The first step to overcoming your own personal obstacles to networking is to realize that it is time to revise and reframe your definition of networking. This will help you develop an entirely new approach and attitude that has the added advantage of addressing many of your concerns. The first step toward revising your definition of networking is to review a list of what it is not.

Networking is not:

- Thrusting yourself or your card in front of as many people as possible
- Meeting and greeting as many people as you can
- Giving your "elevator speech" in 20 seconds so that someone will "buy you"
- Only targeting people you think can do something for you
- Developing a gigantic database of names
- Something that is short term
- Only about promoting yourself
- Picking somebody up or flirting
- Instant rapport
- Love at first sight

Exercise: *Recognizing Networking Turnoffs*

Think of the reasons why you have not followed up with most of the individuals who have thrust a card into your hand.

- Were they too pushy?
- Did they move too fast?
- Ask too much of you too soon?
- Make promises they could not keep?

Write your reasons here.

_____

_____

Take a look at this list. You may recognize that many of these actions have one element in common: They are essentially selfish and one-sided.

This leads us to the most important element of your new approach to *expert networking*.

If you change your paradigm of networking from an activity valued for what you can get out of it to an activity whose rewards are based on what you can give, you will be well on your way to success.

CHAPTER 3

Overcoming Networking Obstacles

Perseverance is a great element of success: if you only knock long enough and loud enough at the gate, you are sure to wake up somebody.

—Henry Wadsworth Longfellow, Author

I can't! I'm not naturally good at it!

That's what most people say when they describe their networking abilities. Many people believe networking is innate, that you are either born with the ability to talk to people or you aren't. But, skill in networking is not the result of a gene. It is a skill that can be learned and honed.

Networking is more like gardening. You read about it, you think about it, you plan it, and then you practice it. Just like gardening, networking can be learned and perfected. Think of networking like planting a "relationship seed." If properly planted and carefully nourished, with time and attention, it will flourish.

Networking is a seed to be planted and nourished.

And, like cultivating a garden, after the seed is planted, the network takes time to grow, but seeds that receive too little water and fertilizer will probably die.

Overcoming Your Fear of Rejection

Have you ever said or thought, *I'm afraid of approaching strangers*?

Many of us fear approaching strangers, initiating conversations, or calling people in our network because we anticipate rejection. This is entirely understandable, because our psycho-physiological makeup is such that we do everything in our power to avoid pain. And rejection is just that: pain. In fact, as noted previously, studies have located the sites of the brain where individuals experience physical pain as the same sites where an individual experiences the psychological pain of interpersonal rejection.

It is human nature to want to prevent oneself from experiencing pain. On a subconscious level we avoid situations that expose us to feelings that cause discomfort. For most people, this is the greatest inhibitor in reaching out and building new relationships.

Consider: How many times have you stopped yourself from making a connection based on one or more of the following questions:

- What if they are not interested?
- What if they do not return my call?
- What if they turn away when I approach them?
- What if they respond in a way that makes me uncomfortable?

These are absolutely normal fears. Nobody wakes up and says, "Please expose me to pain." Consciously or subconsciously, you are conditioned to avoid situations that may cause discomfort. As renowned life coach Anthony Robbins says, 99% of people are paralyzed by fear. The key to *expert networking* is to join the one percent of people who have overcome their fear.

The same principle applies to approaching a stranger, arranging a meeting, or going to a networking function. It is vital that you recognize the urgency of exposing yourself to those situations, because the benefits far outweigh the disadvantages.

You do not have to be an extrovert to be an *expert networker*, but you do have to be willing to take risks and cope with possible rejection. As

Susan Roane points out, "You'll never know if the person sitting next to you could change your life if you don't speak to them." Or, as Rick Frishman puts it more bluntly, "You might be standing in line next to your future husband or the person who will give you your next job. Call it luck, call it fate, but you can't call it anything if you don't open your mouth and say hello."

To look at it another way: If you don't even try, you just rejected *yourself*. Now *that* should be your biggest fear. And while you're at it, commit to memory these powerful words by Eleanor Roosevelt: "No one can make you feel inferior without your consent."

It is also important to recognize that networking relationships do not have to develop into deep and lasting friendships. If anything, a wide variety of informal acquaintances can be more professionally advantageous. In her studies on social networks, Bonnie Erickson found that individuals who had a wide diversity of acquaintances were often more successful. Employees with varied networks got jobs with higher ranks and greater incomes. The reason for this, she discovered, is that "acquaintances" that are *less* like each other are *more* likely to have new information, *and* are more likely to include people who can and do influence hiring decisions.

Erickson says

> Thus family and close friends provide fewer jobs than do people outside the intimate circle. More highly placed people generally have connections to higher-placed jobs. An advantage of having varied connections is an improved chance of knowing such a useful contact. Another advantage of diversified connections is their value to a future employer, who often wants people with varied connections that the firm can use.

Like a high diver who takes a deep breath before taking the plunge, there are strategies you can utilize to both recognize and transcend your fears.

Dealing with Your Inner Child

One way to overcome feelings of rejection is to recognize that we can all have deep-seated "inner child" reactions to social situations that involve rejection or conflict. Kip Williams is an Australian psychologist who specializes in the psychology of ostracism and rejection, and even he found himself experiencing that pain.

I was at a park with my dog and suddenly a Frisbee rolled up and hit me in the back. I took it and looked around. There were two guys playing, so I threw it back to them thinking that I'd go back to my dog. But then they threw it back to me. So then I threw it to them and they threw it to me, so I sort of joined their group, and we were throwing it around for a couple of minutes.

And then, all of a sudden, they stopped throwing it to me and they just threw it to each other back and forth and back and forth. I was amazed at how bad I felt so quickly, and I also felt really quite awkward. Finally, I just sort of slithered back to my dog, and if it weren't for the fact that I was a social psychologist, I think I would have felt worse still.

Williams was experiencing that "nobody wants to play with me" pain, which we all were probably exposed to at some point in our child-hood. His strategy for overcoming the pain was to adapt the experience for use in the laboratory by measuring an individual's neural response to the perceived experience of being excluded from a game. Our response as adults embarking on the road toward *expert networking* is to remind ourselves that it is our inner child who fears rejection. We, on the other hand, are grown-ups, and have probably already survived numerous and varied experiences of rejection. It is always the inner child who is concerned that perhaps "no one wants to play with me," but, as adults, we have the ability to rationalize and counsel ourselves. The worst that can happen is that you will hear the word "no," but adults can and should develop the skill not to take it personally.

Exercise: *Recognizing Your "Inner Child" Reactions*

An important first step to overcoming "inner child" reactions is to become aware of them. In the following exercise, circle the response

(A, B, or C) that best describes the action you would normally take in each situation.

1) You are shopping in a crowded supermarket and discover that another shopper has walked off with your cart. Would you...?

A) Rush up to the shopper and demand the return of your cart

B) Simply point out to the shopper that she has taken your cart, and acknowledge that she made an understandable mistake in the crowded supermarket

C) Offer to help the shopper find her own cart and while you are both looking, start a conversation about the difficulties of shopping for groceries on the weekends

2) You are at a school function and notice an empty seat at a table. Most of the people at the table appear to know each other already. When you take the empty seat, the other people at the table carry on with their conversations. Would you...?

A) Clam up, feel miserable, and count the minutes to the end of the event

B) Decide this group of parents is clearly not interested in newcomers, get up, and go in search of somewhere else to sit

C) Pick up the plate of cookies on the table and offer them to the others

3) You and a colleague are the leading candidates for a new position. The colleague gets the promotion instead of you. Would you...?

A) Feel deeply humiliated and lay low for the next week

B) Let other co-workers know that you felt the decision

was unfair to gauge their reactions

C) Make a point of congratulating your colleague, and offering your support

If you identified more closely with "A" responses, then your "inner child" is doing most of the reacting for you, and you will need to work a little harder on your networking skills. If you picked mostly "B" responses, your networking techniques are developing, but could do with more honing. If you picked mostly "C" responses, you are well on your way to being an *expert networker*.

Exercise: *Talking to Your Inner Child*

When somebody does not treat you the way you would like to be treated, or is unfriendly, or you feel you have been unfairly treated, you have to remind yourself that you feel, on some level, as if *nobody wants to play with you*. But, you also have to remember you are an adult, and have the ability to remind yourself not to take it personally.

Step 1: Think about a time in the last couple of weeks when you were upset or irritated, or felt in some way you were dismissed or rejected.

What kinds of feelings did you have?

_____

_____

Can you identify the "inner child" feelings that may have been evoked? How many of these responses do you remember from your childhood when you were treated unfairly or rejected? Add a few of your own, if you like.

- Someone stole my toy!
- Nobody wants to play with me!
- They didn't choose me for the game!
- They're picking on me!
- They're laughing at me and calling me names!
- But I *didn't* break the vase or spill the milk!
- It's not fair!

Step 2: Now that you have identified your "inner child" responses, you can dialogue with yourself and write down a more "adult" reaction. Remember, you are a grown person with the gift of being able to take the initiative and, if necessary, the power, to walk away from an unpleasant situation without taking it personally.

Don't Take Things Personally

In *The Four Agreements: A Practical Guide to Personal Freedom*, the Toltec Sage, don Miguel Ruiz, writes that we shouldn't make assumptions and shouldn't take things personally. "Nothing others do is because of you," he writes. "What others say and do is a projection of their own reality, their own dreams.

When you are immune to the opinions and actions of others, you won't be the victim of needless suffering."

We project our feelings and beliefs onto other people. So, when you are treated rudely or dismissively by an individual you are trying to get to know, it is natural to assume that the person is reacting to you. However, it is frequently the case that this unfriendly, cold, or, frankly, rude individual is caught up in his own thoughts, feelings or problems. One useful strategy in these kinds of situations is to say to yourself, *Happy people are nice, and unhappy people are unkind!* I even go so far as to tell myself that someone who was unresponsive to me may be in terrible pain.

I have so inculcated this into my children, that if someone at school was nasty to them, they frequently expressed more concern about the emotional state of the child who treated them badly than they did about their own hurt feelings. I am proud to say they have carried this habit into adulthood with them.

Realizing the extent to which people who are cold and rejecting are often expressing their own negative feelings can enable you to achieve a necessary distance from this kind of challenging interpersonal situation. Ask yourself, *What's the worst that could happen?* Although our inner child may be wounded and feel like "they do not want to play with me," or "they don't like me," the advantage of being an adult is the capacity to realize "it is not about me."

As you change your paradigm, you'll start realizing that if you don't get the desired response, it's not necessarily personal.

Once you understand that the pain of fear is a factor for most people, except for the very few who acknowledge it, you will be able to dialogue with yourself and take action despite the fear. If you do that you will be amazed at how much easier it is to remove the fear. Moreover, if you do not take rejection personally, you will find it easier to perceive the situation differently and, therefore, open yourself up to countless networking opportunities.

Motivate Yourself to Move Forward

There's an old saying, "He who wants milk should not go to the pasture and *wait* for the cow to back up to him." Besides overcoming the fear factor, there is another consideration. Surely everyone is familiar with another popular saying: "Nothing ventured, nothing gained." This is an attitude that will certainly help you on the road to *expert networking*. Yes, rejection and pain are possibilities. But they are a small price to pay, considering what you would lose if you don't initiate conversations and develop relationships. Surely the pain of never getting the job is greater than the fear of calling on someone. Ask yourself, *What do I have to lose by reaching out compared to the potential gains?* Remember,

if you ask for something, you may not always get what you want, but if you don't ask at all, you absolutely won't get it.

Use the promise of success and of future benefits to motivate yourself to take chances. You will find that there will sometimes be rejection, but there will also be plenty of acceptance. Keep in mind that you only need one parking place, one job, and one spouse at a time. In other words, relax. You don't need to become *everyone's* best friend, so let go of the pressure to have a meaningful interaction with everybody you meet.

Be honest with yourself about your fears. There isn't a magic formula that you can apply, and suddenly you'll stop being fearful. There's not going to be some magic wand waved over you that causes you to suddenly shout, "Now I'm a brave person!" It doesn't happen like that. Rather, you can become a person who can take a little more pain. Tell yourself: "I don't love doing this, but I'll deal with it, because it's going to take me to the next level." It is easier to *act* your way to feeling better, to temporarily put on the mask and do what it takes to be proactive, than it is to change the way you feel about new social interactions.

Keep in mind, as well, that overcoming fear will be its own reward. As you start to feel better about yourself as a proactive (rather than passive) person, you will be ever more ready to take on more challenges. And, yes, you will be less reticent about speaking to strangers who could become potential resources.

Don't Be Afraid to Speak to Strangers

Bill's Story: *While waiting for an appointment in the lobby of a large food service company, I introduced myself to James, a sales-man who was also in the lobby. I learned that he was demonstrat-ing his blenders to 70 food service representatives at an upcom-ing sales meeting. I asked what product he was going to use, and he said he hadn't decided yet. I offered the use of my company's mixers if he would be willing to pass out a flyer.*

Instead, he invited me to give a talk to the representatives my-self, giving me a lot of valuable exposure, and also saving me the company fee. In the future, James intends to use my company's mixers when demonstrating his blenders, and he will pass out a flyer for the mixers when doing so. He even said he would gladly pay for them. If I hadn't made the effort to introduce myself to a stranger, this would not have happened.

When you confront your fear and do it anyway, not only do you over-come the fear, you also feel good about yourself. Mastering something you previously feared can be deeply satisfying and fulfilling. As Susan Jeffers says,

"Feel the fear and do it anyway."

IT'S NOT ABOUT BEING PUSHY

Networking is only perceived as pushy if you believe networking is strictly about receiving. I challenge you to develop the mindset that *expert networking* is more about *giving*. And it is more about *contributing* in some way, whether small or large, to the people you connect with. Not because, as the Bible says, it is better to give than to receive, but because it is also easier on your ego. Most people feel more comfortable if they are in a position of giving a favor, rather than asking for one.

So why is it about giving? Well, what happens when you give? You are in the driver's seat; you become the resource, the person who holds the power, the *go-to* person, someone people need to know. You become a worthwhile investment. You can only be perceived as pushy if you are only in this pursuit for yourself. Roane calls this type of person a "networking mongrel." Once you understand that *expert networking* is a form of *mutual* interaction, you'll learn to frame requests and approaches in a way that is not perceived as pushy.

Your best relationships are those that have been built slowly over time. You don't have to be a social butterfly. Sometimes I go to an event and just sit at a table. I don't run around the room trying to meet people. I simply sit at my table and see what results from having interaction with the few people sitting nearest me.

Similarly, I could walk into a cocktail party where there are 50 people. I would never try to meet all of them, but I will talk to and create a relationship with one person, maybe two. I will feel no urgency and I will not go into that room with a sense of pressure. I do not do the "card thrust," because I know that meeting 50 people is meaningless. The only thing that's meaningful is the one person I happen to connect with.

Another very effective strategy that has the advantages of both helping to overcome your fear of approaching strangers, and putting you in control of the situation, is to think of every situation as if you were the host of your own party. Take charge and initiative. If you were hosting your own party, you wouldn't wait for introductions to be made. You would try to make sure all of your guests feel more comfortable by facilitating conversations. You'd introduce one guest to another. You would do your best to make sure everyone relaxed and enjoyed themselves.

Remember, most people feel exactly the same way you do. You have the added advantage of being more conscious of the *expert networking* process.

Starting a Conversation

"Don't knock the weather; nine-tenths of the people couldn't start

a conversation if it didn't change once in a while," said humorist Kin Hubbard

You're not going to meet new people to add to your network if you don't talk to them. Frishman says, "You might be standing in line next to your future husband or the person who will give you your next job. Call it luck, call it fate, but you can't call it anything if you don't open your mouth and say hello." Starting a conversation with a stranger can be daunting. However, it can be less intimidating if you approach starting a conversation in a relaxed way, with the understanding that sometimes you will get a response. If you don't get the response you desire, there are always new connections to be made further down the road. Think of the process as one of:

A *connection* + A *conversation* = A *collaboration*

Making the Connection

The wonderful thing about first making a connection is that it gives you an opportunity to test the waters. Start off casually. You never need to start a conversation by introducing yourself to or sharing your job title with the other person—that can come later. Instead start a conversation by making a comment about your surroundings, the level of noise, or the décor. You may even compliment the other person on what they are wearing and ask them where they got it. Greatly original? No! But, do these simple comments work as conversation openers? Why, yes!

Look around you for ideas. Check out the room or meeting hall. Is there something that can trigger a conversation with the stranger standing next to you? Is there something interesting about the room, or is there an attractive painting on the wall?

If you're in a place where there is nothing concrete to talk about, you can always use the food or drink as a starting point. Avoid a comment that can only elicit a "yes" or "no" response, such as, "Isn't the food good," as an opener. Rather, try something like, "This fish reminds me of trips I used to make to the shore." This kind of comment will hopefully prompt the other person to ask you questions in return. Open-ended questions allow people to elaborate, and this creates conversation. You are drawing the person out and helping them become part of a conversation.

Continuing the Conversation

Once you have launched into a conversation that will hopefully lead to a collaboration, there are some basic strategies you can use to keep the conversation going. To start with, it is important that you avoid asking too many questions. The person you are talking with should not feel as if he or she is being interviewed. Quickly asking a lot of questions will only make the other person feel uncomfortable and leave them looking for a way out of the conversation before it has really begun.

Humor is always helpful. You don't have to be a stand-up comedian, but telling a funny story can help break the ice. You'd be surprised how sharing something humorous that happened to you will get others to open up. Everyone loves to laugh, and laughing makes people feel comfortable. This is a surefire way to lighten up the tension and get people talking.

Make the other person comfortable by giving them the opportunity to choose a topic. Also, be careful not to invade their personal space. Stand far enough away to give them breathing room, but close enough to be able to clearly hear them.

Pay attention to the messages you're sending out with your body. Are you frowning at the room in general with folded arms? Are you standing rigidly with a pasted-on smile, looking like you're frozen to your spot? If so, you're sending out very clear signals that warn people to steer clear of you because you're just not interested in engaging with them.

It may go without saying, but put in the extra effort to actually *listen* to what is being said. Award-winning keynote speaker, author, and business and executive coach Don Yaeger says there is a major difference between listening and hearing, and you will put yourself in a position of advantage if you recognize what differentiates the two. He says

Listen, don't just hear, Hearing is a sense. Listening is an act. It requires attention. Listening requires us to slow down and not be building a defense to what is being said while it is being said. That ability to be a person who can listen in moments of challenge will set you apart because few people do it, and it will allow you the opportunity to grow more quickly.

> *I once had an entire conversation with someone walking the bridge into the CNN Center about how badly equipped Atlanta residents are for cold weather. My brief comment to Jill about not having the right attire...THE CONNECTION... Started an entire CONVERSATION. We then agreed to meet for coffee downstairs at the CNN Center sometime, and exchanged cards.*
>
> *The next time it was really cold I remembered our conversation and called Jill, asking her if she would like to meet for coffee. That was the start of a long and fruitful COLLABORATION, as Jill turned out to be a video editor, who has since edited many of my tapes for presentations. I have now become an endless source of freelance work for Jill, and I have an experienced editor in my contact list. And this all started with a comment about the weather!*

Doing Your Homework

If you're not sure about the interests of the people you're about to meet, it's a good idea to check on the nightly news before you head off to the party. General knowledge and an understanding of breaking news issues provide great conversation starters when all else fails. If you haven't had time to stay up-to-date on current affairs, some knowledge of the latest celebrity gossip can also help break the ice.

Do some research beforehand if you're going to a professional function that represents a networking opportunity. Prepare some conversation starters that convey the impression that you are knowledgeable about others' fields of interest. If you are prepared to deliver plenty of opening lines, and have trained yourself to ask open-ended and appropriate questions, you will quickly find that the art of conversation is much easier than you would have ever imagined.

One thing that is very helpful in making conversation, if you haven't had time to research someone is to remember that *everyone* has three things in common...a PAST, a PRESENT, and a FUTURE. You can have an entire conversation with a person by keeping this in mind.

> *When I had to interview a champion middleweight boxer on the radio, at only a moment's notice, this framework of PAST, PRESENT, and FUTURE came in very handy.*
>
> *There I was, live on radio, when my producer said, "Nadia, you have ten seconds to air." What do you ask when you've done no research whatsoever and are not a boxing fan?*
>
> *Well, first he has a PAST: "When did you first know you wanted to be a boxer? When was your first win? Who inspired your boxing career?"*
>
> *And he has a PRESENT: "Now, what fight are you currently training for? What is a day in your life like in this phase of your career?"*
>
> *Finally, he has a FUTURE: "Tell me, what does the future hold for you? Whom would you like to fight that you haven't as yet? At what age will you think enough is enough?"*

The interview went very well, and my producers were impressed. With these three simple hooks in mind—past, present and future—an entire conversation can flow.

Not everyone is a middleweight boxing champion, but most people will respond if you ask them where they were born or moved from, what their current challenges and experiences are, where their children go to school, or inquire about their goals and aims.

Remember, to start a conversation, you do NOT need to immediately introduce yourself; you can simply start with a comment or an observation. This takes the pressure of rejection off. The other person will likely respond to your comment. If they don't, nothing is lost. It's like saying "hi" to a stranger you pass on the street. If they respond, it's fine, but if they don't, it's no big deal. But, if your casual comment leads to a friendship and/or a networking relationship, you have gained a lot.

CHAPTER 4

Become a "Go-Giver"

The universe operates through dynamic exchange; giving and receiving are different aspects of the flow of energy in the universe. And in our willingness to give that which we seek, we keep the abundance of the universe circulating in our lives.

—Deepak Chopra, Author

Instead of being a so-called "go-getter," one of the most powerful *expert networking* tools you can develop is to become a "go-giver." So often you go into a situation focused on what you can get out of it immediately, rather than what you can give. This kind of attitude can be detrimental because *expert networking* is as much about *giving* as it is about getting. Think of it as making a long-term deposit in the favor bank of life, and rewards will follow, because when you give advice, or provide leads the recipient will likely feel an automatic investment, and a desire to return the favor.

Being a go-giver creates the environment for mutual reciprocity. It is a prime example of the universal law of sowing and reaping. Knowing that you are helping someone else as much as, or perhaps even more than, they are helping you makes networking a lot less scary and gives you more confidence in your own networking abilities.

"Go-Giving" in Action

For a clearer idea of how becoming a "go-giver" can help overcome your own inhibitions about networking, consider the following example.

I recently gave a class at the Turner Broadcasting Professional Development Center where Brian, one of the attendees, worked for the Atlanta Braves. At the start of the class, Brian said he always found networking difficult because he hated to be "needy" or to ask for a favor.

A couple of weeks after the class, he related to me how changing the paradigm had helped him. Instead of approaching a potential new employer with a What can you do for me? attitude, he went into the interaction thinking, I am in a great position to be helpful to you. I am young, enthusiastic and energetic. I am also eager to benefit from your many years of experience in the field. *In communicating both his energy and willingness to learn from his potential new employer, he realized that by asking for advice or guidance he was "giving" the potential employer respect and acknowledgement.*

Being helpful to other people does not always need to be a concrete action. You can be equally helpful by acknowledging other individuals' achievements, and giving them a chance to offer advice.

For example, a question such as, "Mr. Smith, you have been very successful in navigating the world of sports management. Do you have any ideas on how I should proceed?" recognizes his success by respecting his input and opinions. (Note: This approach is not a demand, but a request.)

Keep in mind that **networking is a privilege, not a right.** Rick Frishman emphasizes that this attitude should become a way of life, not an "occasional tactic." He says it is vital to establish a wide reputation as a person who is genuinely eager to help out and who does not set others up simply to get something in return. Networking is about learning to be selfless, to be helpful and generous.

Of course, like any investment, the payback might take time, but it will come, one way or another. What you are working on is a long-term, hopefully lifelong, connection.

I have truly experienced the rewards of generous, patient networking myself, as illustrated in the following experience:

As a new arrival in Atlanta, I signed up with a formal networking group to meet people and make contacts. While I didn't get any leads that resulted in a job, I did meet a friend, Kate, who had a freelance marketing company at the time. After a year, we both decided to leave the group, but we continued to meet regularly for lunch. During one of these lunches, Kate mentioned that she had just met Nancy, the president of a communications company, who hired external consultants. She arranged for the three of us to meet.

At the time Nancy was working on a book and did not have any immediate work. She did, however, mention that her son, who had lived in Mexico, was interested in broadcast journalism.

I volunteered to meet with him to see if I could provide any guidance. After meeting with her son, I offered to pass his resume on to Eric, a colleague of mine at CNN International, who was responsible for hiring writers. I also gave him my advice on what was required and an excellent book on broadcast journalism. Of course, it helped that he was a skilled and talented writer. He was hired, and is thoroughly enjoying his career in the CNN newsroom.

Eventually, Nancy did have an opportunity for me and I have continued to work for her as a presentation skills trainer ever since. Nancy is now an essential member of my network. We are two people who are mutually invested in each other's success. The fact that I went "out of my way" to assist her son helped to further solidify our relationship. My friend Kate, who made the first contact, remains an integral part of this network. Nancy and I feel indebted to her for the introduction and we both continue to look out for marketing opportunities for her burgeoning business.

Two questions I am often asked are:

- I can certainly give to someone who needs something I have to offer. But how do I give to someone who does not need me?
- How do I give to someone whose expertise, advice, or contacts I need?

The answer is simple: giving comes in many forms.

Exercise: *What Do YOU Have to Give?*

A useful strategy is to develop a self-inventory to determine what you bring to the table for your network. This includes your talents, natural attributes, skills, acquired capabilities, values and objectives that you consider important. For example, Benjamin, an ambitious young college graduate starting out in the working world, could list his attributes as:

- Smart
- Energetic
- Resourceful
- Flexible
- Available

Ben approached a high-powered executive, and offered to document the company's history in exchange for mentoring. As a result, he had access to each and every person in the company, and interviewed many of them. With this kind of access, he was able to learn about a vacancy in the company and lobby successfully for the job.

So, what do YOU bring to the table (or, the organization, group, forum or committee that you want to join)?

Step 1: List all of your attributes below.

_____

_____

Step 2: To the right of each word you wrote, give an example of an instance where you were able to successfully apply that particular attribute.

Respect and Acknowledgment

As mentioned above, you can also "give" to someone by showing respect for their guidance. Most people are very willing to share their wisdom, if the question is framed in a way that acknowledges them. This gives the other person recognition and validates their success.

Experiment with these questions, rephrasing them for your situation:
- Mr. Wilson, you have been so successful in positioning yourself in the company. I am at a crossroads. How do you suggest I proceed?
- Jeanette, you have navigated your career with great success; do you have any suggestions for me, starting out?
- Cameron, you've been such a help in providing me with career guidance. Is there anything I can do for you?

I have also learned in the world of networking (as in the case of Nancy) that while the president of an organization or the head of a department may not need your help, she may have a relative, a son, daughter, niece, or nephew, who does.

How do you obtain this information? The answer comes from the father of networking, Dale Carnegie, "You can make more friends in two weeks being interested in other people, than in two years trying to get them interested in you." Take time to connect with people and work at becoming a great listener and a good conversationalist. Ask a lot of questions about *them* (their outside interests, their passions, and of course, their family). Afterwards, make sure they know who you are, and what you do, and that you are open to assisting them in any way you can.

Change the Radio Station

For your mind to work like an *expert networker*, you will be thinking every time somebody says something to you. You will think, *What can I do? How can I help? What resources do I have?*

Instead of being constantly tuned into WIFM (what's in it for me), you change your radio station to WIBU (What's in it for both of us?)

I was once asked to lunch by a young woman who wanted to talk to me about media training. Without taking a breath, Heather asked me how she could get started, how I got my clients, and what a training session should consist of. At no point during the discussion did she offer me anything in return for my "intellectual property." Had she been more astute in the art of networking, Heather would have said, "Nadia, you are an experienced media trainer, but I have lived in Atlanta all my life. If I find us the clients, would you like to partner with me?"

You see, Heather has the vast Atlanta database, and is very well connected, but she didn't leverage that. Instead, she came across as a pushy, WIFM/WCIU (What's in it for me, where can I use you) person. She demanded, rather than requested, and as a result she alienated a potential source of information, resources, and possibly work.

Exercise: *Becoming a Strategic Resource*

Find a cooperative friend or acquaintance who has not previously been part of your network to test your new paradigm before you launch into *expert networking*. Try it at home, or better yet, with a friend. In classes when we have practiced the exercise, people have found everything from new jobs to housekeepers. Once, someone even found a plastic surgeon!

Brainstorm with each other. The following are some useful questions to start:

- What do I know?

- What do I have?

_____

_____

- Whom do I know?

_____

_____

- Who is in my network already?

_____

_____

- How can they be helpful to this "new" member of my network?

_____

_____

Remember: Expert networking is about giving, sharing and caring. It is as much about being a go-giver as it is about being a go-getter.

CHAPTER 5

Building Your Online Network

Technology does not run an enterprise, relationships do.
—Patricia Fripp, Keynote Speaker & Executive Coach

Harnessing technology to grow your network is an absolute necessity in this day and age. Research that would have taken days or weeks in the past is now available at the click of a button. There is an online networking organization or special interest group for every imaginable topic, instantly allowing us to connect with like-minded individuals across the globe.

As much as technology has added to the convenience and ease of outreach, it is in no way, shape, or form a replacement for real human interaction. Online networking should be viewed as a *tool* or supplemental resource to your networking efforts, not as something that exists in a vacuum. While the internet can link us to more people than ever before, it is best viewed as a jumping-off point and not as the end-all-be-all of networking interaction.

From Click to Connection

How you approach your online network takes as much skill as your in-person network. Everything you've previously learned applies. As with traditional networking, the biggest mistake people make is that they go into an online relationship with a "what's in it for me" mentality. Career development expert Stacy Pollack says

Some of the best professional relationships I have today are with people I persistently reached out to and convinced them to chat with me. At the time, I had nothing to offer, but I reached out as my authentic self, looking for help and advice. Everyone had been where I started at one point in their life and could relate. Now, I have more professional pull with my blogging and my position within my organization, and I can return those favors to people who have helped me in the past. There is always an angle you can find to get people to talk to you! Sometimes you just need to get creative.

You may think you don't have anything to offer the other person, but you do have a network of people as well as your enthusiasm and attitude of appreciation. When reaching out to someone online for the first time, **craft your customized introduction very carefully with a "what's in it for both of us" message.** Once you've launched an online relationship or started the conversation, be sure to circle back to them frequently to see how you can be a resource for each other.

If you know the person is interested in a specific topic or lifestyle, send them an article with a note, "I saw this, thought you'd be interested." This isn't stalking; it's appreciated following. The human brain is wired in such a way that we thrive on being appreciated and having our views reinforced.

My mantra is that if you approach the world with the attitude that you want something from the situation, but you are aware that there should be value for the other person too, you will be more successful in person and online. The challenge when approaching someone online is to break through the noise and overload of information constantly being tossed through the screen. Online networking is also much more sterile and impersonal than in-person networking, so you need to be even more aware of how you present yourself.

I had a young person reach out to me online. She told me she'd watched my YouTube videos. She asked if I was available for a quick cup of coffee to see whom we might introduce each other to in our respective industries. She's an entry-level person, but she still has access to people. She made sure I knew this in her introduction.

My new acquaintance also asked me for guidance, and offered to help me as well. Now we've embarked on a mutually beneficial business relationship and even a friendship.

Digital Dos and Don'ts

According to Gary Burnison, author of *Lose the Resume, Land the Job*, as many as 25 percent of job applicants are unsuccessful because of the way they have presented themselves on their social media pages. "If you aren't careful," he advises. "You can tweet yourself out of a job."

It's well established that anything posted to an online social media network or website has an eternal shelf-life. While you can carefully craft your personal image, one angry rant or photo that casts you in a negative light can severely damage how you are perceived online and, thus, as a person.

How many stories have you read about politicians, celebrities, and other notable individuals who fell from grace as a result of something they posted online? Once information is out there for all to see, it can wreak havoc on your personal brand if you aren't constantly thinking about the bigger picture in terms of how you are portrayed.

The recent reboot of the television show *Roseanne* was abruptly cancelled by ABC after namesake, Roseanne Barr, made offensive tweets. She deleted them following the backlash, but the damage was already done. Social media gave her unlimited access to the masses, but it also proved to be her undoing.

Indeed, the internet is a double-edge sword. It can connect us in ways we never thought possible, but one false move and our reputations can suffer irreparable damage. Pollack cautions

A really important thing to remember is that you also can't hide behind a message. My rule of thumb when talking on LinkedIn is that if this is not a message I would deliver out loud to a person's face, I also would not write it in a message box. Same goes for posting online! Once something is on the internet, it can't really be erased, so make sure you are thoughtful in any message you put out there.

It is absolutely imperative that your online image reflect who you are in the very best light.

One mother I know tells her teenagers they should not post anything they would not be comfortable with their grandmother reading or viewing. It's important to remember that perception becomes reality, and the way you present yourself online can be either an advantage or a detriment.

The highways of social media have become so overcrowded that people's capacity to find you, and for you to find them, is getting more and more difficult. So, the ability to harness, finesse, and master these skills is more important than ever. This requires constant, consistent effort. Don't be a slave to social media, but do schedule a time each week to scour your online connections for those you may want to convert to an in-person relationship. You may have recently heard someone speak at a symposium and wish to request they meet you for a cup of coffee to bring your interaction to the next level.

Before you request that meeting, though, you want to make sure your social media is updated and professional. In the same way you will look potential contacts up online, they will try to find out more about you. You have a greater chance of your request for a meeting being granted if you are easy to find online and your profiles across the "big three" (Facebook, Twitter, and LinkedIn) are maintained in a way that attracts others to you.

Utilizing Social Media for Networking

According to Pollack, "Digital networking is in no way a replacement for in-person connecting, but often it's the pre-work needed to land those in-person opportunities." In fact, a 2016 survey on LinkedIn found that 85% of jobs are filled through networking contacts.

Following are some excellent steps to connecting online:

- Carefully craft your online profile on key networks.
- Build a list of key people you want to connect with and follow them on social media.
- Subscribe to relevant blogs and newsletters.
- Connect with influencers on the big three: LinkedIn, Facebook and Twitter.
- Share influencers' posts on Facebook.
- If you meet an influencer at an event, take a photo that you can post on social media and "tag" them.
- Email a compliment regarding a recent achievement or milestone.
- Research an influencer you'd like to meet to find common ground.
- Offer to make an online connection with someone from your network.
- Write a meaningful endorsement for a connection on LinkedIn.
- Conduct quick, periodic "check-ins" with key individuals.
- Follow up an in-person meeting with a thoughtful email.

Social media should be about sharing advice, guidance, and resources. It should not be used purely for self-promotion. People who self-aggrandize run the risk of becoming annoying.

Your goal is to get people to like you, trust you, and want to do business with you.

The Big Three

Unless you are completely new to the world of online networking, you are probably already aware of the three major resources for online connections—LinkedIn, Facebook, and Twitter. But, are you using them to your full advantage? Let's take a look.

LinkedIn

If you don't already have a profile on LinkedIn, it should be your first priority for increasing your professional presence online. It is the world's largest online professional network, with more than 562 million users in more than 200 countries. If you were to pick one resource that would maximize your online networking reach, this would be it.

In addition to giving you space for a personal profile, LinkedIn offers a plethora of tools and resources regarding every topic imaginable. The site utilizes both free access and paid upgrades so you can tailor your experience to meet your needs. You can also link to a personal website or blog and share recent accomplishments with your followers. In short, LinkedIn is very much a one-stop shop in terms of establishing your personal online network.

The key thing to remember with LinkedIn is that, unlike other social networks, this one is professional in nature. This is the place to hone your business profile, tout your skills, endorse the skills of others, search for jobs, and conduct research on your area of expertise. It is NOT a place to post photos of your recent family vacation, tell jokes, or pass along entertaining viral videos.

Facebook

More than two billion users flock to this social media hub each month and, chances are, you are already one of them. While not a professional network per se, Facebook offers seemingly endless outreach opportunities and the chance to connect with virtually anyone and everyone. But because it is primarily a social network, you'll need to be mindful of your individual activity and how you are perceived online.

You can actually streamline your Facebook presence into both a personal and professional version. By editing your account's privacy settings, you can control who has access to your personal musings versus your professional posts. This is a very useful tool in terms of managing what you'd like specific individuals to see.

Here, you can also find specific personal interest groups on every imaginable subject. Search for related groups by topic or browse the groups your friends have joined. There are so many options, it's easy to get overwhelmed by the sheer volume of available resources. While you can join as many groups as you wish, do try to isolate those in which you'd like to get personally involved through discussions and posts.

The biggest pitfall with Facebook is the tendency to minimize the importance of online professionalism and etiquette. Bear in mind that the image you portray can cause people who do not know you well to make assumptions about you. The access Facebook allows into our daily lives is unprecedented, and when not used thoughtfully, this can be very detrimental to your professional profile. Many people have lost out on job opportunities and networking relationships because of the way they chose to present themselves on this easily-accessible platform.

Twitter

Limited to postings of 280 characters, Twitter is a social messaging platform that allows for quick communication on a mass scale. Tweets, as they are called, can be public or private, or within a select group. Through Twitter, you can follow influencers or post interesting links or personal knowledge. While direct messaging is available through Twitter, most tweets are public and shared en masse.

You can share the tweets of others by retweeting. Label your tweets with a particular hashtag (using the "#" symbol) to group tweets together, create buzz around a specific event or topic, or start a conversation. Twitter is a simple way to stay in touch, share quick thoughts and keep yourself relevant with your contacts.

In terms of networking, it isn't so much about the number of followers you have, but rather, the type of community you build. Twitter can be a less threatening way to reach out to an influencer because the platform does not allow for as much depth as other social media sites. It's a place to share your thoughts and promote the thoughts of others in a very public forum. Unlike other platforms that require you to first be accepted by individual users you follow, Twitter gives you access to anyone you choose. You can locate people to follow based on their names or key search words relating to a particular topic.

Beyond the Big Three

Once you have established a presence on LinkedIn, Facebook, and Twitter, there are many other online resources you can use to further grow your networking reach. The list is endless, and your niche interests will help you further define and clarify what groups best suit your individual needs. Online Meetup groups can be a great place to start and provide the perfect segue to linking your online and in-person presence.

Pollack suggests keeping a spreadsheet of the conversations you have with people you meet online who have been helpful to you. Follow up sporadically with the contacts on your spreadsheet to thank them for their help and to check in with them. "This helps turn random connections into meaningful and long-term relationships and sometimes friendships," she says.

Remember to always play the long game when it comes to networking. Just because someone can't help you today, doesn't mean that somewhere down the line they won't be able to! Treat everyone with respect and try to foster relationships by nurturing all your leads.

As with all networking, nurturing your online network takes time and effort. A deep appreciation goes hand-in-hand with building a long-term, meaningful relationship. Write someone a genuine recommendation on LinkedIn, rather than simply clicking on pre-provided endorsements. This is an excellent way to nurture and give back to the people you want as allies. A clicked endorsement means very little, but once someone writes something genuine and authentic for you, you've started a relationship.

If you are going to a meeting, look the participants up ahead of time to see what they are interested in and who they are connected with. Don't underestimate the power of showing genuine interest. This may seem obvious, but far too often we overlook the obvious or choose not to apply it. It's not enough to apply it just once. What sets a good network apart is the consistent application of these principles.

Just because you've sent someone a LinkedIn request and they are now part of your network does not mean they are a genuine part of your active alliances. Yes, you've taken the first step. But, just like putting a plug in a socket, you now have to turn it on and nurture the relationship.

If you don't hear from the person online, don't get discouraged. You can follow up with a similar type of message, again, as a way of keeping in touch. Like everything else, this is a numbers game, and some people will never respond. Don't take it personally.

As much as these online resources can help us, they can also send us off on unrelated tangents that distract us from our original goals. Don't be a slave to social media. Schedule a time each week to scour your online connections for those you want to convert to an in-person relationship. Send them an email inviting them for a cup of coffee to take your discussion offline.

As I stated earlier, do not think of your online interactions as a replacement for face-to-face communication. Social networks are great places to *start* the conversation, but it's up to you to elevate it to the next level.

Here's an example of how you might approach someone via email or through social media channels:

> I was fortunate enough to have heard you speak at the [insert event] and was truly impressed by your thoughts on [insert specifics related to your skills or interests]. Your experiences were especially insightful because I am also interested in [insert reference to specific career or personal goal] I know your schedule is limited, but if you would allow me to treat you to a cup of coffee, I would welcome the chance to continue this conversation and discuss how we may be able to work together in the future.

Exercise: *Practice Online Networking*

Aside from the big three, make a list of niche online groups that may be helpful to your online networking efforts.

Make a list of individuals who would be helpful to you and how each should be approached online.

Choose one person you want to reach out to online and craft your customized "what's in it for both of us" introduction message.

_____

_____

Make a priority list of individuals from your online network whom you would like to meet in person, along with a time line to schedule those meetings.

_____

_____

CHAPTER 6

Strengthening Your Networking Confidence

Nothing is so contagious as enthusiasm; it moves stones, it charms brutes. Enthusiasm is the genius of sincerity, and truth accomplishes no victories without it.

—Edward Bulwer-Lytton, British Politician and Author

There is no doubt that you are much more effective, and have a greater chance of attracting people to you and generating the kind of response you want if you exude confidence. Positive energy attracts and negative energy repels. This is especially true in networking.

First, you have to believe in yourself—then you are in a position to communicate your sense of confidence to the other person so that they believe what you have is valuable. In this way, you are able to radiate a "Life is good to me, would you like to know my secret?" attitude that will work wonders by attracting rather than alienating people.

Are there people in your life you cannot bear to be around because they have that "negative persona"? Be aware of the level of energy you are exuding. You may not even be conscious of moments when you are in a negative state, nor even be aware that other people can see it, and that you are sabotaging yourself.

I learned this the hard way. When I first left South Africa, I thought it was important for every single person I met to know how traumatic it was to emigrate. I thought everybody I met should know what terrible pain I was in. So I'm meeting some-

body and I'm telling her about the agony of leaving, and all the great things I have left behind.

Susan looks at me, and I will never forget what she said, "Nadia, I think you've a very nice person, and I think you've very talented, but I can't work with you."

"But why?" I asked, quite stunned.

Susan said, "Because you're in too much pain."

At the time I thought, What an unkind person. *But you know what? She wasn't my best friend. I hadn't developed a relationship with Susan where she would care. And basically, she didn't want to take on all my problems. In retrospect, I understand her position very well.*

Create a Positive Emotional Memory Disc

One of the best techniques to radiate positive energy and overcome self-doubt is the creation of your own Positive Emotional Memory Disc™ (PEMD), a "disc" of positive memories you keep stored in your brain so you can recall them as needed.

Focusing on past successes and recalling a positive feeling enables your body to automatically relax and respond.

Reflect for a moment on memorable moments of triumph you have experienced. These memories can be anything from the exhilaration of winning that tough competition to capturing a scholarship to your dream school to interviewing for and landing that perfect job.

Once you have your own original catalog of positive memories, it is vital that you constantly "refresh" your disc with newer, more recent positive experiences, so that your memories are immediately accessible. It should become an essential part of your thought process, and eventually quite effortless.

"File" these memories as you would file your music on an MP3 Player. "Carry" them with you as your reservoir of confidence tools to draw on when you need them. The goal is to relive these experiences in all their glorious detail and commit them to memory where they can be pulled up as easily as your next appointment on your smartphone.

Overcome Self Doubt

On occasions when I need to evoke wonderful feelings of enthusiasm and confidence, I reflect on hosting the Women in Film Awards with Alfre Woodard. I can clearly see the red dress I was wearing, and I can recapture the feeling of joy as she complimented me on a job well done. I can still see the audience, hear the applause, and taste the champagne that was served.

I clearly remember accessing my PEMD when I was auditioning at Georgia Public Television (GPTV) for a show called Homes for Better Living.

An hour before the allotted time, I had received a phone call from a superior who berated me for a perceived error and who did not give me any chance at all to explain myself. I had only been in the United States for a few months. I was devastated and convinced that my career had been ruined. This was not true, of course, but I didn't know it at the time. So, after collapsing into tears, I braced myself for the audition.

As I was driving downtown, I remembered to access my disc, my reservoir of positive emotional memories. By simply recalling that moment of triumph at the Women in Film Awards, I was able to defuse the humiliation and feel less traumatized.

The second I arrived at GPTV, I was called into the room and asked by the producer to recall the script. In my emotional

state, I had overlooked even glancing at it, and told the produc-
er I would rather improvise.

I looked straight into the camera, and gave a wonderful de-
scription of a silver and white Christmas. It worked! I got the
job, and the following week, the pilot of Homes for Better Liv-
ing **aired.**

I had a choice when I went into that audition. I could have told them my sad tale of woe, which may have gotten me their sympathy, but definitely not the job. The decision I made, to walk in with confidence and exude positive energy, is what made me successful.

Exercise: *Burn Your Own Positive Emotional Memory Disc*

Take 10-15 minutes to write down at least three positive, personal experiences that validate, enforce, and remind you of your abilities. These experiences should evoke feelings of confidence and triumph.

_____

_____

After you have written down these experiences, describe how they made you feel at the time.

_____

_____

Write down at least three positive attributes you feel these memories reflect.

_____

_____

Now, imagine three situations in which it would be helpful to access your PEMD and write them down.

In a book called *Mind Power*, John Kehoe writes that while most people believe they are only as good as their last experience, that is just not true. We are a combination of all or our successes. Just because you're having a bad day, doesn't mean all your past successes just go away.

Sometimes you need help with that positive vibration and sometimes it's automatically there. If it's taking a day off, what can you do?

One very effective "mind trick" is to think about how famous Olympic champions prepare for the dive of a lifetime. How do they do it? When it's time to do the dive, to psyche themselves up, they "play a video" in their heads of the perfect dive. Then they stand on the diving board and *visualize* themselves performing this perfect dive, as they've done before in other competitions. Finally, they execute the perfect dive.

Sometimes you just need to remind yourself how successful you've been, and it's particularly helpful on days when you're going through a confidence low.

Positive Self-Talk

According to French novelist, Honore de Belzac, "Nothing is a greater impediment to getting on well with other people than being ill at ease with yourself." Our inner dialogue—what we communicate to ourselves—has a huge impact on the way we project ourselves in our outer world. So often it is our subconscious negativity that sabotages us. While this is probably not news to you, we all have to be reminded to be conscious of all the negative messages we send ourselves. If we change our thinking, we can learn to avoid the mire of self-destruction.

Ask yourself the following questions:

- Am I clear on my intent?
- Am I conscious of exactly that I want to say?
- Am I giving myself a positive outcome?
- Am I excited about my content?

All too often we allow our state of mind to reflect in our attitude. We forget that sometimes all we need to do is act like we are up, even when we are feeling down. That little strategy alone can get you over most hurdles that come your way.

CHAPTER 7

Building Rapport & Relationships

When dealing with people, remember that you are not dealing with creatures of logic but creatures of emotion.

—Dale Carnegie, Writer and Lecturer

As the Atlanta-based sales and presentation guru Ken Futch so wisely points out: "We all have a primary style of operating. While it is important to know our own, the power comes in understanding how to relate to other personality styles."

Futch is right.

We obviously resonate and connect more with some people than with others. Each and every one of us relates to people differently. Some of us are very open and share personal details quickly. Others are more reserved and would never think of discussing our personal lives upon first meeting. There are those people who leave a meeting having noticed the tension that existed between two colleagues, and there are those so focused on the task at hand that they would never notice.

What are you...?

- A leader or a follower
- Reserved or open
- Introverted or extroverted
- People-focused or task-oriented
- Rational or intuitive
- A thinker or a feeler
- Sociable or a "loner"
- Empathic or unaware of other people's emotional reactions

How to Treat People

Dr. Tony Allesandro, a highly respected motivational and marketing expert, is one of many observers who says one of the most important keys to building successful relationships is developing an awareness of other people's relating styles. "It is only by understanding the nuances through which other individuals see the world that we can begin to relate to them in a meaningful way," he notes. "When you treat people the way you want to be treated, you create relationship tension; when you treat people they way they want to be treated, you build rapport."

Treat people they way *they* want to be treated.

To relate to people more successfully, it is important to learn how to read their verbal, vocal (voice inflections), and visual signals, and then adapt your behavior to accommodate their behavioral style. Some individuals find it easy to converse with strangers, and will quickly share relatively personal information. Others are more reserved and may need time to feel comfortable in a new social situation before opening up. While the more open person would probably enjoy a personal interaction that is warm, lively and open, the more reserved individual is likely to shut down and "head for the hills" if approached too quickly.

Individuals with different personality characteristics also prefer different kinds of communication styles. For example, people who have strong leadership qualities usually appreciate direct, results-oriented communication. Creative types, on the other hand, might respond well to communication that refers to their field of interest. They may not be interested in details, but will appreciate being given time to plan and accomplish their own work.

Meanwhile, introverted, detail-oriented individuals are less likely to respond well to overenthusiastic behavior they feel impinges on their personal space. This kind of personality will probably prefer to be given as many details as possible, and appreciates time to gather information and decide on solutions.

Some people value interpersonal relationships; others are more comfortable as "loners." While a person who is invested in interpersonal relationships may value expressions of appreciation and support, a "loner" may feel uncomfortable in that kind of situation, and prefer a certain distance. It is important to be sensitive to individuals' needs for interpersonal validation.

Expert networking is essentially a form of marketing yourself. Knowing your personality type, as well as recognizing others', will give you a distinct advantage.

Understanding Personality Styles

Allesandro has identified four basic business personalities:

- Directors
- Socializers
- Relaters
- Thinkers

Director

A *Director* is results-oriented, decisive, and direct. This personality type is likely to say things like, "I want it now!" This personality style is highly focused on productivity and achievement. This is the person you want on your team when you need to dig in and get things accomplished. On the flip-side, this style of leadership can sometimes be off-putting or come off as domineering.

The best tactic when working with a Director is to be direct yourself. Speak in terms of goals and facts and limit conversations to the task at hand. Be a problem solver and strive to work with them efficiently and professionally. To work well with a Director, you must remember they like to be in the driver's seat and you are best served taking on an assistant's role.

Thinker

The *Thinker* prefers to be given as many details as possible, and appreciates time to gather information and decide on solutions. This networking style is careful, detailed, reserved, and relies heavily on research. As a result, a Thinker can sometimes spend too much time thinking and get caught up in the minutiae of data and statistics, sometimes losing sight of the end goal.

When working with a Thinker, organization is key. Come to the table prepared and be willing to back up your findings to show that they are valid and related to your overall goals. Make every effort to work methodically and accurately. Thinkers can move at a slower pace, but they are practical and value structure and attention to detail.

Relater

The *Relater* is likely to be friendly and to avoid conflict. This personality style values expressions of appreciation and support. This personality type is valued for his listening skills and for going the extra mile to really get to know people. A Relator takes time to get to know people, often resulting in the formation of a truly authentic relationship.

Because Relaters exude warmth and friendship, they are often sought out by others and are pleasant to work with. However, they sometimes run the risk of being so agreeable as to avoid any and all conflict. As a result, they are often poor decision makers who will mask their true feelings in an effort to maintain their likable persona.

Socializer

A *Socializer* is enthusiastic, creative and more likely to say something like, "I've got a great idea!" This personality type is not typically detail-oriented but they do appreciate freedom to plan and accomplish their work. Those with this personality type are often creative, charismatic, and spontaneous. Unlike the Thinker, a Socializer is not overly concerned with research and data. As a result, they can sometimes play fast and loose with facts, so colleagues must make an extra effort to check for accuracy.

The Socializer is typically a quick and decisive worker who enjoys interacting with others. They appreciate hearing everyone's ideas and working together as a group. A Socializer thrives on the process and often cultivates an atmosphere of inclusiveness. For these reasons, it's also important to be sure everyone is clear on the end result since this can sometimes get bogged down in opinion and discussion. Putting things in writing can go a long way toward clarifying goals and making sure everyone is on the same page.

Expert networkers consciously adjust their language to adapt to those with whom they are working, and even plan the best way to start a conversation. While you are working on this skill, remember that the essence of good conversation is to communicate to the other person that you truly understand where they are coming from. Remember, people don't care what you know until they know you care.

Exercise: *Interacting with Other Business Personalities*

Write down your personality or style.

Think about a person outside of work with whom you have a relationship. Based on his or her personality traits, explain how you have or have not gotten along with the person.

_____

_____

Think about an important person at work you get along with. What kind of business personality do they have?

_____

_____

Try to identify some of the ways you communicate and work with this person. Do you think you have adapted your relating style to this person?

_____

_____

Identify a person in your work environment you have trouble relating to. What kind of business personality does this person have?

_____

_____

Based on what you now know about the four business personalities, what could you do differently with the people you have identified to create more harmony?

_____

_____

To accelerate your communication skills, redo this exercise with different people in mind who exemplify each of the four business personality types.

Relating to Another Personality Style

I am an extrovert, and a person Dr. Allesandro would call a *Socializer*. If I only networked or connected with people I felt an instant rapport with, I would be tremendously limited. I am often so caught up in connecting with people that I don't have the time or forethought to wonder beforehand if I am going to get along with someone. I simply reach out to them and see what happens. Being a Socializer has often paid off in ways I couldn't imagine.

When I first met Nancy Neill, the president of Atlanta Communications Group, she was very reserved. If I did not have the knowledge that her reservation was part of her PERSONALITY STYLE, I would have mistaken it for being standoffish and may not have persevered with our conversation.

But I was able to identify that Nancy was the kind of person who is initially guarded, a THINKER. My realization that she operates differently than the way I do meant I needed to take the interaction more slowly than I naturally would. I knew Nancy needed to assess the situation, whereas I was impulsive. As a result of my patience and understanding of her different operating style, we have become great friends, and I have had the pleasure of working with her many times.

The more you are aware of another person's business personality, and how it corresponds to yours, the easier networking becomes.

CHAPTER 8

The F.I.R.E. Approach to Networking

There is nothing we like to see so much as the gleam of pleasure in a person's eye when he feels that we have sympathized with him, understood him, interested ourselves in his welfare at these moments something fine and spiritual passes between two friends. These moments are the moments worth living.

—Don Marquis, Journalist

Now that we have covered the basics, it's time to put it all together. Despite what you may think, networking does not require you to be pushy. That's a myth perpetuated by networking groups that encourage attendees to meet and give their card to everyone in the room. Besides, just making a connection is not enough. When we network, we need to become relationship builders. For many people this is much easier said than done. To give you some guidelines, I have developed the **F.I.R.E.** approach to networking.

Feel good about yourself.

Interest in the person you are relating to must be genuine.

Relax and be comfortable with yourself (which will relax the other person as well).

Engage the other person with your energy and enthusiasm.

F.I.R.E in Practice

F – As mentioned in a previous chapter, you have to *feel good about yourself*. And, by this stage, if you participated in the exercises, you've developed the kinds of self-talk strategies and positive memories that can do the trick. Remember, nothing is a greater impediment to getting along well with other people than being ill at ease with yourself. As one anonymous sage pointed out, "Cheerfulness is contagious, but don't wait to catch it from others; be a carrier."

However, if you feel you still need to strengthen your sense of confidence in yourself, please go back and review chapters three and six.

I – It is essential that you show genuine *interest* in the person you are relating to. As Dale Carnegie wrote, "You can make more friends in two months by becoming interested in other people than you can in two years by trying to get other people interested in you."

People want to be valued. Interest is not only shown by what you say, but is enhanced by your eye contact and body language. Of course, you do not want to stare soulfully into the eyes of a stranger, and you definitely want to respect their personal space. You can show interest in subtler ways, by angling your shoulders slightly toward the person, and definitely by giving them your full attention. Do not scan the room for other, potentially more interesting, people while you are engaged with someone else.

We also need to show interest in a way that is most appealing to the type of person we are relating to. There are many names for this ability. Some call it empathy, some call it reading people well, and others call it emotional intelligence. Very simply put, it is the ability to see the world through another person's eyes.

R – You need to be as *relaxed* as possible in all interactions. If you're not relaxed, others will sense your tension and become uncomfortable, perhaps even recoil. There are few things more uncomfortable than the feeling that a person *wants* something from you. There is a feeling of desperation about it. You want someone to be comfortable and confident that this is a long-term investment in a relationship that has the potential to grow and evolve.

I have found that **an easy-going approach eliminates a great deal of anxiety in the networking process.** As a reminder, you don't need to go up to a person and immediately introduce yourself along with your occupation. Rather, start a relaxed conversation based on an observation of something happening in the immediate vicinity. If the person is responsive to you and a rapport develops, then introduce yourself and talk about what you do for a living. That approach takes a lot of the pressure off. Just forget about the titles and talk. In the words of author Alvin Toffler, "The less you need something, the more power you have."

E – *Engage* the other person with a high level of energy and enthusiasm. Nothing sells like enthusiasm, and by radiating positive energy you are far more likely to attract the kind of person you would like to network with. As Ralph Waldo Emerson wrote, "Vigor is contagious, and whatever makes us think you feel strongly, adds to our power and enlarges our field of action." So, this is not the time to let people know you can't stand your current job and are actively looking for a new one. Similarly, don't share the fact that you dislike your co-workers or the neighborhood you live in. Rather, focus on the positives, and communicate the kind of positive energy that will attract people to you.

Active Listening

To be an effective communicator and fully engaged in the F.I.R.E. approach to networking, you must be tuned in to the other person's feelings through *active listening*. Active listening encourages communication and puts other people at ease. Active listening also clarifies what is being said.

Look your interlocutor (the person with whom you are speaking) directly in the eyes when they talk to you, and *maintain* eye contact. Be conscious about not letting your mind wander. If you realize you have been thinking about the day's to-do list, catch yourself and bring your focus back. Focusing on a conversation is more difficult when you are in a noisy room with live entertainment or televisions on the wall. Avoid looking at those things that could distract your attention. Sit with your back to distractions or move to another part of the room if necessary.

Be aware of body language, both yours and the other person's. For example, do not look at your watch or shift around in your chair. Focus on what the other person is saying, rather than on what your response will be. Smile slightly, but do not laugh loudly. This way, you won't look like you're trying too hard to please.

Let the other person have his or her moment.

Do not try to one-up them with your better joke or a worse experience. Listen closely and do not interrupt the other person, except to ask clarifying or qualifying questions like, "How did it make you feel?" Reflect back to the other person by rephrasing what they have said. This will make it clear that you have understood their message. When possible in the conversation, pay specific and sincere compliments. Be careful that you don't resort to false flattery, as another good active listener will see right through it, and you will ruin your credibility very quickly.

Genuine interest is a powerful thing. As renowned poet Maya Angelou maintains, we don't always remember what someone says, but we remember the way they made us feel about ourselves. Sometimes with friends I make a point of listening and asking questions that help me understand more fully what they are saying. It is always tempting to try to bring the conversation back to your own concerns. It takes discipline and self-awareness to give your full attention to the other individual, but if you do so, they will feel that you are really listening to them.

CHAPTER 9

Casual or Incidental Networking

Every day fishing day, but not every day catch fish.

—Bahamian Proverb

We have defined the true nature of networking and analyzed the factors that may personally stop us from taking full advantage of networking opportunities. We have discussed strategies for projecting a sense of confidence, developing rapport, and relating to different personality types.

Now we will look at situations where you can put this knowledge into practice. The general rule of all of this is: *Network most when you need it least.* Or, as Harvey Mackay, author of *Swim with the Sharks Without Being Eaten Alive*, says, "Dig your well before you're thirsty."

One common scenario is the casual, incidental networking opportunity. These are moments such as your child's soccer game, the hairdresser, or the company cafeteria, when a brief connection develops into a conversation. It is these kinds of moments that can sometimes evolve into a collaboration, and you never know when or how you might meet someone whose life can impact yours.

The Importance of Developing Rapport

The question at hand is: how does one light the F.I.R.E., or build rapport, in a casual or incidental networking environment?

How many times have you just met someone casually while standing in line at the ATM or at a restaurant, while watching a game, or at a company party? How often has this type of brief connection developed into a conversation? How often, still, has this evolved into a collaboration?

Take a moment to think of the many opportunities you have every day to mingle, meet, and converse with someone new. For me, a simple stroll on the bridge from the parking lot to the CNN building has resulted in many conversations, which have led to a second meeting, and finally turned into a collaboration. It was because of such a chance encounter that I met CNN Promo Producer, David Tooch.

One day, as I was walking along the bridge, a young man happened to be walking a few feet in front of me. I simply commented on his rather unusual backpack, which had Hebrew lettering on it. As we neared the end of the bridge leading into the CNN building, I asked him which department he was with. He said, "Promos," and that gave me the opportunity to ask if they ever needed voice talent. Enthusiastically, he said, "We certainly do," and gave me his card. I now do regular voice-overs for the CNN International Promo Department. It didn't end there.-

During one of my voice-over sessions I learned about the CNN Guest Bookings Department and was encouraged to apply because of my networking and communications skills. Now, as a freelance Editorial Guest Producer, I identify and book experts around the world to appear on CNN International.

Another reason casual, incidental meetings can be invaluable is because you just never know where they can lead.

The person you meet may know the person you *need* to meet.

When I first arrived in Atlanta, I was sitting in a packed downtown restaurant. The tables were so close together that my chair was literally touching the next table. It was my comment about this to the friendly lady whose chair abutted mine that started us chatting. She heard my accent and asked where I was from, thus launching a lively conversation about how cosmopolitan Atlanta was becoming.

Only later did we exchange names and cards. Ney Lawson (by now I had found out her name) and I arranged to have lunch at the same restaurant a few weeks later. We realized after our initial connection that we both had a lot in common. For example, she was an art collector, and my husband and I have an extensive collection of South African art. Ney was also an instant hit with our children and soon became what I now refer to as our "Fairy Godmother."

It was a year or so later, when I was having a conversation with executives at Coca-Cola, that my relationship with Ney could be defined as a networking one. Coke was looking for a speaker for their mentor program. They were looking for someone "preferably female, preferably someone very high-profile...like Carol Mosley-Braun." Within 20 minutes I had Carol Mosley-Braun herself booked as their next speaker.

You see, Carol and Ney are longtime friends, and had been in touch throughout Carol's career as she transitioned from being a lawyer to serving as Ambassador to New Zealand. Because of my relationship with Ney, I had the privilege of accessing her vast network, and Carol was a part of it.

But, when I met Ney, did I think, *Is this a good contact?* No. I thought, *This is a nice person.*

I try to have my "What can I do for you?" antenna switched on whenever I have these chance encounters. But, given their brief nature, it is not always easy. That is why you must *first* develop rapport. You build a connection that says, "This seems like a person who would be nice to get to know better." *Think about the endless people you have met who seem interesting, but subsequently faded out of your life because neither of you followed up and developed a what-can-we-do-for-each-other relationship.* When people fade out of your life, you never get the benefit of having real access to each other's network.

I recently found myself at a dinner party sitting next to the CEO of a major electronics company. He was someone who had the potential to be a good contact for my business. I knew nothing about him, but based on the PAST, PRESENT and FUTURE frame, I asked him, (PAST) "Did you always know what you wanted to do?" And, "When did you land your first deal?" (PRESENT) "What are your current challenges? And your frustrations?" (FUTURE) "Do you have any exciting new projects planned?"

With that, an entire conversation ensued, and later I was able to arrange a meeting and discuss the various programs I offer. This resulted in several coaching sessions for his management team as well as a keynote address at his annual board meeting. All this transpired because I was mentally prepared to engage him, or anyone else for that matter, in a comfortable conversation.

As you can see, these principles can be applied to any conversation as long as you apply the F.I.R.E. rule. First, *feel good* about yourself, and then show genuine *interest*. Be *relaxed* in your approach and *engage* them with your enthusiasm.

Conversation Starters Based on Past, Present, and Future

Past

- Where are you from, originally?
- What school did you go to?
- How long have you been here?

Present

- What do you do for fun? (Interests? Hobbies?)
- What do you enjoy about your job?
- Where do you live?
- How do you like your neighborhood?

Future

- What's next for you?
- Do you expect to live in your town for the rest of your life?

At a Mixer or Formal Networking Event

- How long have you been with the company?
- Where have you worked before?
- What do you do for the company?
- What projects are you currently working on?
- Are you planning to stay in this job?
- Where do you see yourself in five years?

I never go up to someone and formally introduce myself, then start talking. I keep it as casual and nonchalant as possible. And I've almost always found that most people are ready to have a little chat.

Keep your introductions as casual and nonchalant as possible.

Places to Strike up a Conversation

- Your child's soccer field (other parents)
- Grocery store (waiting in line)
- Cafeteria (sit with a different group)
- Parking garage (waiting for the valet)
- Airport/airplanes (that person sitting next to you)
- Company picnic (during a softball game)
- Coffee Shop (their interesting book title)
- City park (while walking your dog)
- Bookstore (while browsing)
- Art gallery (in line for the free wine)
- Library (at a special event)
- Sporting events (those seated around you)
- Volunteer events (a local neighborhood clean-up, or tree planting)

Starter Phrases

- I am always amazed that they have so little staff at peak hour!
- I can't imagine my life before Starbucks.
- This is the first flight I've been on this month that hasn't been delayed.
- Do you think it could get any colder/hotter in here?
- I love shopping here; this market always has the freshest-looking produce!
- I see you're getting [book title], have you read any of [the author's] other books?
- I'm really impressed with this gallery's new artist; the way [the artist] mixes colors is almost magical.
- Great service here—I get the feeling the valets are secretly Olympic sprinters.
- This is my favorite dog park. What breed is yours?

Topics Easy to Be Nonchalant With

- The weather
- The parking situation
- Fashion
- School
- Natural disaster in the news

- Traffic
- Commuting
- The service
- The décor
- Local happenings

Be wary of making comments on topics that can be polarizing such as politics, religion, or American foreign policy. People can have very strong views on these kinds of topics, and you may find yourself in a heated discussion with an individual you do not know well.

On the other hand, if the other person shares their opinions *first*, and your views are similar, then these subjects can be optimal for building rapport.

It's Your Party

Another extremely useful networking technique in both casual and formal networking environments, such as a cocktail party, is to play the role of host or hostess. I call this the attitude of,

"It's my party, and I will introduce myself to others if I want to."

Try it. You will be surprised at how effective this can be.

For example, the next time you are at a social event, rather than waiting to be introduced, make the introductions yourself. If you observe two strangers standing awkwardly next to each other, engage them and make introductions ("Hello, have you two met?" Or, "Oh, do you two know each other?"), as if they were guests at your party. In this way, you'll learn their names, and earn their gratitude for helping to break the ice.

Remember, in both casual and incidental networking opportunities, your life does not depend on it. You do not need to formally introduce yourself. You can make a relaxed comment like, "Can you believe how many tables they fit in here?" Or, "Is it always such a long line?" Or, on a positive note, "Can you believe how good the service is here?" The point is, by making a casual comment, you can initiate the conversation and then determine if you want to introduce yourself by name and continue the discussion.

In the same way that champions in sports practice visualizations, you can do something similar. This will help you approach your next chance encounter with confidence, rather than fear. By now, you should be able to answer the following questions in the affirmative.

- Am I at ease with making conversation and with my general social skills?
- Am I taking advantage of every opportunity to meet someone new?
- Do I approach situations thinking, *I never know whom I might meet*?

As Henry David Thoreau wrote, "If one advances with confidence and positive energy in the direction of one's dreams and endeavors to live the life which he has imagined, he will meet with success unexpected in common hours."

Entrance Strategies

Sometimes you will walk into a room where you're on your own because everyone seems to be engaged in conversations with each other. There is apparently no host for the evening and no one is making introductions. How do you enter into a conversation already in progress between two or more people?

Keep in mind that people will react to the energy you exude. This is where the "it's my party" attitude will come in handy. People love confidence, and if you approach any conversation-in-progress like you are very comfortable in your shoes, they will instantly warm to you. Again, don't introduce yourself right off the bat. Make a comment that they can respond to, such as:

- Man, the traffic was bad coming from the North, how was it for you?
- Have the formalities started yet?
- Have you tried the buffet yet, and is there anything you recommend?
- I'm going to find the bar. Can I get a drink for anyone?

When Networking Is Not Worth the Effort

In his seminal book, *Emotional Intelligence*, Daniel Goleman makes the point that personal qualities like self-discipline, self-awareness, and empathy are as vital to success as a high I.Q. Indeed, one of the most important skills an *expert networker* can develop is finesse—or being able to "read" people's reactions. The skill here is recognizing whether or not your networking "target" is interested in the relationship.

For example, notice their body language:
- Are they facing you, or looking away?
- Are they responding to or blocking the conversation?
- If it is two or more people, are they talking *around* you and not *too* you?

Exit Strategies

If someone is not responding to your efforts to initiate or to continue a conversation, you'll probably want to remove yourself from this uncomfortable situation. Don't worry about hurting their feelings. If someone clearly does not want to have a conversation with you, don't torture yourself, or them. Move on. But here are some exit lines to make it a little easier:

- I'm going to go and get a drink, would you like me to get you anything? (If they say no, just say, "Nice meeting you," and make your exit.)
- It was really nice to meet you, let me give you a card.
- Please excuse me, there's Jack Smith, and I really need to talk to him.
- Lovely to speak with you, enjoy the evening.

The "Bookmark" Strategy

What if you're in the middle of a conversation and you see someone else you want to meet, but you still want to develop the relationship with the person you are talking to? Say something like:

- I need to talk to Maxi over there before she leaves, but I really want to finish what we were talking about.
- That was really interesting information you shared with me. Please give me your card, so I can follow up with you soon.
- A colleague of mine has a lot of expertise in your field, and I know you will enjoy meeting each other. Let's all plan to get together.

Exercise: *Make Your Own Inventory*

Take a few minutes and make a mental inventory of your everyday activities. I'm sure you'll realize that your daily life is a cornucopia of casual or incidental networking opportunities. Go over the list of possible venues that come to mind, and write down those you think could provide opportunities for you as you go about your day. (And make sure to take advantage of them in the near future.)

Remain in the Driver's Seat

Acting as your own hostess, having a list of conversation openers and planning for the sometimes necessary exit strategies will allow you to remain in the driver's seat as a true *expert networker.* Ways to stay in the driver's seat:

- Request, rather than demand, access to people.
- Do not limit your networking to people you perceive as powerful (or you will quickly get the reputation for being selfishly expedient).
- If you are in a conversation, don't scan the room for the next person to approach.
- Walk into your relationships generously. (There are people who try to claw their way to the top, and these kinds of people may get ahead, but they rarely stay ahead.)
- Approach people without invading their personal space. (Give them room to breathe.)
- Don't make requests before you begin to understand a person and forge a solid connection.
- Don't offer more than you can deliver or more than you feel comfortable delivering.
- Don't be too attached to the outcome. (This increases your anxiety

and undermines your confidence.)
- Take it slowly. (Show that you have patience.)

The best networking opportunities happen when you are not tense, anxious or in need.

If you need to build up your confidence, you can even practice these skills in situations where you have nothing at stake—like at a neighborhood party. At the very least, you could make a new friend, and you never know what kinds of networking rewards you may get.

Remember, if you bear in mind that everyone has a PAST, a PRESENT, and a FUTURE, you will never run out of topics for a conversation.

CHAPTER 10

Formal Targeted Networking

There are no shortcuts to any place worth going.
—Beverly Sills, Actress and Singer

How do you develop relationships and alliances without being labeled as "pushy"? How do you go about strategically getting into a situation where you have a better chance of arranging that meeting or seizing that opportunity? This is what is called *targeted* networking—networking for a particular purpose. Your purpose or target is to gain access to the right people, the right opportunity, and the right connections in your industry.

The first thing you have to do is become involved. In other words, show up and bring all you have to the table. The next requirement is to have something of value to bring to the network. "It is vital," writes Rick Frishman, "that you obtain and maintain expert knowledge in a particular area."

Bring It All to the Table

To "show up and bring all you have to the table" means picking a few important places to spend your time and really becoming involved so others will see your commitment and want to invest in you. Being involved in a forum or a group (preferably as an active board member) is one of the best things for you to do, so people associate you with the organization and get to know you.

Use networking events productively. *Expert networkers* pick one or two networking groups related to their profession or hobbies and start attending their meetings. To meet people, you could find the event's organizer and ask to be introduced to a few key people. Get involved in the group, even in the areas that aren't glamorous such as setting up a meeting or picking up trash afterward. This is a great way for people to get to know you, see your commitment, and want to do business with you.

Formal Networking Venues

The key to networking on this level is *access*. And the way to obtain access is to comfortably find people through your everyday and community-based activities with whom you share common interests.

Here are some examples of networking venues you will find in most communities:

- Mentoring programs
- Annual picnics
- Business resource groups
- Volunteer programs
- Boy Scouts/Girl Scouts and Big Brothers Big Sisters
- Your children's activities
- Booster clubs or school alumni organizations (Hearken back to your college days and get involved with the clubs established around your alma mater.)
- Rotary (Many *expert networkers* recommend joining rotary because a lot of very influential, powerful people often belong. Rotary events give you the opportunity to meet others on an equal level. Similarly, a group like Women in Technology is useful, even if you are not actually working in technology.)
- Wine tasting associations or book clubs
- House of worship (church, synagogue, mosque, temple)

As mentioned in Chapter 5, the internet has made it much simpler to reach out to individuals who previously would have been far out of reach. For some, it may be easier to hide behind a computer screen than to initiate networking relationships. Do not fall into this trap! Your computer is a fabulous tool to help you with initial outreach, but it cannot replace an eventual, in-person connection or the building of a long-term, authentic relationship.

Darrah Brustein began her career in the fashion industry and later became an entrepreneur, launching a successful credit card processing company with her twin brother. At a certain point, she realized her generation was largely missing the tools and skills needed to make meaningful contacts outside their own social circles, so she launched networkunder40.com, a networking site for the under 40 crowd that now reaches more than 30,000 people and has regular programs in four U.S. cities. While this online meeting place is an ideal starting point, Brustein cautions against the idea that the computer has replaced the need for human interaction. She says

> People use the digital component like a crutch, and I feel very strongly about the importance of creating in-person connections. This generation is so addicted to being online, and while I think of LinkedIn and Facebook as tools to connect, most people think that's all they need to do.

Digital and in-person connections need to find a way to collaborate.

Be discerning! You don't need to belong to 100 different organizations. Rather, get involved and become well-known in one or two carefully chosen organizations. A very good strategy would be to join one work-related and one community-related organization so that you are raising your profile within your company, but also ensuring access to outside connections.

Venues that relate to your professional interests are particularly valuable. For example, a Georgia-based-journalist could go to Atlanta Press Club events. A speaker could get involved with the National Speakers Association. An accountant might join the American Institute of Certified Public Accountants. And, an executive in the hospitality industry might consider the Food and Beverage Association. These profession-based affiliations will help to increase your visibility within the association, and enable you to become greater than the sum of your individual parts. They also give you the opportunity to leverage the skills you have outside of your job.

You should also consider getting involved in programs within your company. As previously mentioned, Coca-Cola has the Executive Assistants Forum, and Turner Broadcasting has affinity programs, like Turner Women Today. Company forums are an excellent way of raising your profile, particularly if you are active on the board, thus giving you access to people in the company you would not have otherwise.

Volunteer—Early and Often

Bonnie Erickson says the key to broadening one's social networks is through *volunteerism*. "When you join a voluntary association, you get to meet people who have something in common with you, and you also get to meet people who aren't exactly like you." Thus it's a great way to meet a wide variety of people. Sometimes it is also a great way to get to the power players you want to meet.

Readers of the society pages and celebrity magazines have surely noticed that many of the glittering events featured are fundraisers and benefits for a huge range of causes. I want to let you in on a little secret: while the individuals who take part in these events have many commendable motives for participating, they are also taking advantage of the priceless networking opportunities these functions offer.

Indeed, volunteering is an activity that offers multiple benefits. You will be contributing to a worthy cause, like beautifying a neighborhood, or raising money to help fight a serious disease. You will also be enriching yourself, both by adding another dimension to who you are, and by gaining access to people in a special way that creates a feeling of camaraderie for everyone involved.

It is much easier to meet people when the focus is not on you, but

on a cause you are working together to benefit.

If you and the senior executive you desire to have access to are both working on a neighborhood cleanup or hanging drywall for Habitat for Humanity, the social distance and barriers that usually make access to an individual difficult are definitely diminished. You will also have a priceless opportunity to show off both your abilities and commendable personal qualities. And you may be able to leverage your encounter into a more formal networking contact later.

How to Find Volunteer Opportunities

Volunteer opportunities abound within the realms of work, family, neighborhood, city, and the broader environment. Most large corporations offer a wide range of volunteering opportunities, from joining fundraising walks to offering professional expertise to not-for-profit organizations. A good friend of mine who is a tax accountant, for example, helps elderly people fill out their tax forms at a local senior center. Taking the position of captain of a fundraising walk is also a great way to raise your profile in the company.

If you are the parent of school-aged children, then you are probably well aware of the numerous volunteer opportunities available, including tutoring and fundraising activities, like bake sales and seasonal events. Most educational institutions are happy to welcome volunteer help. The advantages for you are: an opportunity to make contact with other parents and a chance to learn more about what is going on at your child's school.

There are also volunteer opportunities with organizations that serve young people, like the Boy Scouts of America, Girl Scouts USA, or the Big Brother Big Sister Foundation, to name a few.

Neighborhood clean-ups, tree plantings, and block parties are all enjoyable activities that benefit your immediate environment, and also offer excellent networking opportunities.

If you enjoy the outdoors, volunteering with organizations that clean up trash on beaches or maintain walking or riding trails would be in tune with your personal interests. It is also a way to meet people who share a common interest with you, as well as offering networking opportunities. Moreover, if you are really adventurous, you can join a volunteering project in another part of the country, or even in another part of the world. All of these are priceless opportunities to expand both your experiences and your networking realm.

If politics is your bag, there are numerous volunteering and networking opportunities to be had at all levels. This can range from addressing a local issue, like electing a candidate to your local school board, to national elections. Political campaigns are extremely labor intensive. People are always needed to stuff envelopes, make calls, and make the personal contacts that are often key to successful campaigns and candidacies. Along with the chance to further your favorite candidate or cause, you can also take advantage of the many opportunities to expand your network with people who share your political views.

From Local Giving to a Global Payoff

Bonnie Ross-Parker's Story: *I love to network. For me, networking is no different than a stroll along the beach. Just like looking for an unusual shell or stone, I love the anticipation of whom I might meet or the relationship I might create. Networking is my version of a treasure hunt. I like to look for and uncover the unexpected. It was during an after-hours networking event that I met an unexpected treasure.*

I began a conversation with a young woman who was the program director for the Junior Chamber of Commerce of Atlanta. At the time I was looking for new avenues to speak and sell my products, and she was looking for new speakers. When I shared that my expertise was networking, she was eager to book me on the Chamber calendar.

I asked about their budget to pay speakers. She was quick to tell me that they rely totally on the generosity of community talent. I remembered that you never know what can come from an act of generosity, and I did not have anything scheduled at the time, so I accepted the invitation to speak.

As it turned out, I began feeling enthusiastic about my commitment. I imagined 60-75 young professionals eager to learn new networking ideas! Enlightening them early in their careers was certainly worth my time and effort. After dinner I spoke for about half an hour, followed by a Q and A. Participants were respectful, asked great questions, and expressed appreciation for my program.

When the formal part of the evening was over, I anticipated one-on-one interaction and book sales. To my disappointment, I only sold two or three copies of my book Walk in my Boots: The Joy of Connecting, *and very few members approached me afterward to chat. The major exodus was to the cash bar inside.*

The program director came by, however, purchased a book, and thanked me for what she felt was a "great presentation." She then told me she hoped the opportunity would present itself for her to return the favor. I felt the connection we made. She had counted on me and I had kept my commitment. Of course, I sent her a written thank you note.

It was several months later when I heard from her. She had given my name to a woman in Nuremberg, Germany, who had contacted the Chamber looking for a suggestion of someone with networking expertise to speak at an upcoming women's conference. I couldn't believe it! Talk about making a connection count!

Three days later I got a call from the director of the German conference. She had already visited my website. She repeated the glowing testimonial she had received, and wanted to check on my availability. Within a short time, I agreed to her very generous terms and a contract was signed.

You never know what can happen unless you make every connection count. My keynote speech in Germany is a powerful example of the opportunities that can result from volunteering your time.

Exercise: *Finding That Volunteer Opportunity*

It is important to volunteer in an area you are interested in, and to be sincere. If you are only volunteering for the networking opportunities, it will soon become obvious, and work against you. Jot down some areas of interest you have or causes you would be interested in helping.

Look around—in your neighborhood, your local newspaper, or on-line—and write down two or three volunteer opportunities you think would be in tune with your interests and concerns, along with the contact phone numbers.

Pick one or two that resonate the strongest with you. Then, make that phone call and get involved. I assure you that if you participate fully and sincerely, before you know it, viable networking opportunities will begin to appear.

Now that you have studied some of the principles of formal, targeted networking, it is time for you to create your own networking plan. You will need to know what you want to accomplish, and to identify the particular organization that can help you reach those goals. Having decided that, you will need to devise a plan for how to access this "hard to reach" person.

Exercise: *Creating a Networking Plan*

Step 1: Define your goals:

- What do I want to do?

- Where do I want to be?

_____

_____

Step 2: Once you have thought this through, answer the following questions:

- Who has the power or authority to help make this happen?

_____

_____

- Who has access to this person (or these people)?

_____

_____

Step 3: Contact the above "access people" and put the wheels for networking in motion.

Serving on a Forum

Bonnie W. got herself out of a dead-end job by joining a forum. Forums are great places for networking and meeting people because everyone is there for the same purpose—to grow and help others grow. Forums often work a lot like support groups, in the sense that members bring up issues and ideas that affect their specific industry or field, and the forum members work together to offer and bring about solutions.

Bonnie W's Story: *I had been with my company for over 15 years, managing to hang on through two re-organizations the* *first part of the 2000s. I had a horrible attitude, and hated my job. Although I was happy to have a job, I had lost my passion.*

I was approached by a friend who asked if I would be interested in working with a team developing a brand optimization for the Women's Forum. I joined the Forum and became an active member. I met several nice people, enjoyed the work, and learned a great deal in the process. My attitude also improved.

One day, during one of our committee meetings, I met Jane. I had no idea who she was, but was extremely impressed with her. After the meeting, I had some follow-up to forward and looked her up. To my great surprise, she had a position open, and it appeared to be the kind of position I was looking for. She is the director of global marketing, supporting some people I worked with in the past, and I would be reporting directly to her. I made a few phone calls to those old friends and then called her directly.

Next thing I knew, I had an interview lined up. I contacted several old bosses and friends for coaching. They were all very excited about my opportunity and helped me immensely. I learned as much as I could in a very short amount of time about the Global Customer Development team, the business model, and their customers.

I've been on the team for more than six months and just love it. I learn something new every day. I'm fully engaged. My passion has returned. And, I always look forward to meeting new people.

Keep in mind that formal, targeted networking takes time. The connections are made when you interact in the same environment with the same people over and over again. It's seeing the same people at your church, synagogue, or mosque so that you almost feel like friends before you actually meet. It's being on the board of an association and demonstrating your values, your deep concerns, or your passions.

Exercise: *Getting Access*

Make an inventory of the forums that are available to you right now. Some may be through your company and others may be available to the general public. If your company does not offer on-site forums, really search one out. Try to avoid the temptation to take the easy route by settling for online forums, which are really glorified Q and A sessions.

True Proactivity

If there is nothing in your community for you in terms of associations or organizations, consider being truly proactive, as entrepreneur Darrah Brustein was. Start your own group on your own terms.

Virginia Bradley also started her own networking group called GlobalEXECwomen. The group connects female executives involved in information technology, and has allowed Bradley to leverage her position to gain incredible access to very important and influential individuals. She is able to approach senior executives and power brokers as a representative of this prestigious group, rather than on her own behalf. The corporate leaders Bradley has approached have been very receptive, because they, too, are interested in the exposure. They welcome the opportunities GlobalEXECWomen gives them to speak, explore, and show what they have to offer.

As you can imagine, when I was once asked to facilitate the group, I was happy to oblige. It gave me the opportunity to get involved with this great organization and meet some wonderful people. Because they were impressed with my performance, I ended up doing one-on-one coaching with some of the participants.

So, do you see how clever Bradley has been? She's created for herself the opportunity to have access to a wide variety of people she can call on when she needs anything.

Create your own forum and rapidly increase your network

She's not asking them for a favor; she is inviting them to be part of the forum. She actually makes people feel privileged to be invited to the group. There are many important people who are beyond the reach of an individual, but who would be happy to accept an invitation to address a group.

Create Your Own Forum

To create your own forum, research the internet. Find other forums already in operation. Get in touch with the person who started the forum, or one of the members. Then "pick their brain" for information. Find out how their forum operates (attend a meeting if necessary). Then devise your own game plan on your terms.

If you aren't ready to launch a forum or professional group, take the initiative to host a dinner party that brings top thought leaders to the table. As the host, be sure to do a lot of preparation to ensure great discussions. This includes preparing questions about what the experts are working on, and figuring out how the experts behave in order to relate to one another. To keep the process of networking and conversation going, make sure many people get the chance to speak. Also, be prepared to change the topic if a particular discussion starts to lose steam.

Exercise: *More on Accessing Those Hard-to-Reach People*

Answer the following questions:

* What forums are available to me now?

_____

_____

* How active am I?

_____

_____

- Is this sufficient to meet new people on a regular basis?

_____

_____

- How high-profile am I?

_____

_____

- How can I leverage my position?

_____

_____

Spend ten minutes brainstorming ideas to get more involved in forums, or how you might create your own. List your notes below.

Network Sharing—Connecting Others

If you do arrange a meeting with someone you see as instrumental to your career advancement, make sure you frame your interaction in such a way that validates and respects their advice. I am always put off by people who DEMAND access to my network. Networking or sharing your highly-valued group of allies is a privilege. It is not a right.

I had an incident recently in which someone called me, knowing I work at CNN, and basically demanded to spend three days with me at my job. She didn't even ask. What she said was, "Nadia, I'm going to be in Atlanta for three days, and I'm coming to see you because I want to work at CNN." She assumed

*she had the right because our parents are friends, and it totally
irritated me.*

*Had she asked differently, I would have been happy to help
her. As it turned out, I did meet with her, but it was out of obli-
gation because of the relationship between her and my parents.
But I did not do any of the extra legwork. Rather than call one
of my contacts with her resume, I just directed her to the Turner
jobs website.*

An approach that is far more likely to get good results is to let the
person you would like to meet know what you are hoping to achieve.
Then ask them if they have a recommendation for how you might proceed. I cannot stress enough the power of *how* you ask versus *what* you
ask. It is essential that you carefully frame the request in such a way that
invites, rather than repels, assistance.

Frame your request in a respectful way. The "How do you suggest I
proceed?" line is a very good one. Also remember that people feel good
about doing good. Always be sure to acknowledge what they have done
for you. Once you have accepted someone's advice, it is essential that
you be appreciative and follow up. (This will be discussed in detail in a
Chapter 12.)

Let others know what a good thing they have done in helping you.

Remember that *expert networking* is a creative process, and should
not be seen as linear. There is no definitive route to where you want to
go. Sometimes it means getting to know someone's executive assistant.
Sometimes it works when you become active on the board of a forum,
committee, or club. And, sometimes, it simply means you strike up a
conversation in the concessions line at the stadium.

CHAPTER 11

Networking with the Power Players

Generally speaking, the great achieve their greatness by industry, rather than brilliance.

—Bruce Barton, Ad Executive

This is the "who I really need to get to" aspect of networking. As you know, it is indeed a challenge to gain access to certain people, such as the leadership in your company, or the CEO of a particular organization whom you would like to approach. But, be assured, it can be done. Try this three-step approach:

Step 1: Know whom you need to get to know.
Step 2: Contact other people who may have access.
Step 3: Find an additional forum to meet them.

The first step of this process, knowing whom you need to meet, is usually obvious. For example:

I wanted to offer my Presentation Skills Program to Delta Technology. I knew the CEO, Curtis Robb, was the decision maker and the person I needed to meet. Simply calling the company and arranging a meeting with him was not an option. First, he does not meet with vendors he does not know. Second, I would come with no references, and my chances of actually securing work were minimal.

With a little research I was able to find out that every year Mr. Robb attends the Women in Technology (WIT) Annual Ball, as Delta Technology is a key sponsor. I offered my services to the

WIT ball organizers as both a volunteer committee member, and the Master of Ceremonies of the evening. I asked Casie Scott Palmer, one of the organizers of the event, to give Mr. Robb some background on me and then introduce us.

As Casie was a member of my network, someone whom I had invested time and energy in, she was only too pleased to reciprocate. Near the end of the event, Casie introduced us. Mr. Robb and I had a short conversation, and the next day, with his permission, I called his office to arrange a meeting. As a result, I have delivered numerous presentations to his organization.

There is also an additional point here in that Casie carried out the ultimate purpose in *expert networking*, that was to arrange for us to meet and then make the introduction. Casie is certainly high on my list of people I want to reciprocate to.

Before you try to reach that important person, do your homework.

Make sure you have a very clear idea of what the person's role is in the company. Also, without transgressing the boundaries of privacy, try to find out a little bit more about the individual. One source may be the company's website, which often provides biographical details about key personnel. It may also be helpful to research recent news and internet sources, which may yield valuable information. For example, if you can congratulate someone on a recent accomplishment, it will certainly help to make a very positive first impression.

Don't Network Empty-Handed

When you are trying to network with anyone, be prepared. You should not be empty-handed, or empty-mouthed (at a loss for words). Rick Frishman recommends carefully crafting your message and approach. Develop a networker's toolkit so you know just what you will say, and so you will have what you need to take action.

Toolkit Items

It is important, whether you are casually networking or being intentional about going after that one person you meet, that you have the items necessary make them agree to a meeting.

- A fabulous sound bite (a great description of yourself and your product or service and how it benefits others)
- Business cards
- An address book or contact list
- A datebook or electronic calendar

Most importantly, be sure you have the expertise to do the job you want to get.

Sound Bite

What do I mean by a "fabulous sound bite"? A *sound bite* is usually defined as a very powerful sentence, or short speech on radio or television. For example, a famous historical sound bite is, "We have nothing to fear, but fear itself" from President Franklin D. Roosevelt's inaugural address.

I'm sure you can think of many more, because good sound bites stick in your mind and make you memorable. That is why it is important to develop your own sound bite, a well-crafted introduction, that will leave a lasting impression on other people. It is a form of personal branding that makes you more likely to be remembered when the search is on for new highly-qualified staff members, or expert services.

In developing your own fabulous sound bite, it is important that you

communicate very clearly what you do.

Think of it as trying to paint a picture in people's minds. Give them an example of what you do, and make it short and tangible. If it is appropriate, you could name some of the skills you bring to your area of expertise and give details of a project that exemplifies the work you do. And, while it is important not to appear boastful, it is fine to give yourself credit for a job well done. Even better, as Peggy Klaus, the author of *Brag! The Art of Tooting Your Own Horn Without Blowing It*, advises, you should start developing a repertoire that consists of your moments of greatest success.

For example, Mary, who is a project manager in the personnel department of a large communications company could say, "I manage large-scale projects that can cause a lot of headaches. Like coordinating the conversion of 8,000 employee IDs into bar codes, which I completed in three weeks." Bill, who is in sports marketing could say, "I work in sports marketing. You know those trendy [famous sports franchise] bobble heads? I got them placed in every sporting goods store in the state."

Business Cards

Have your business cards in hand. Don't make the mistake of having to say, "I'm so sorry, I don't have a card with me." Too many people make this mistake, thinking, "I won't need it at the kid's soccer game today." Yet they meet that one person who would have been a great contact only to lose out on the connection. Even if you are the one who is going to follow up, you want to send your new contact away with something in his hand so he can more easily recall you when you contact him.

To that end, get your picture printed on your business card. A good, professional headshot that accurately depicts who you are and the company you represent will leave a lasting impression on those you meet. Also, keep your business card clean and neat. Do not have so much information on your card that the person reading it has to search for your number. Keep the font large, clear, and readable. White lettering on a black background is fine, as long as the letters and numbers are clearly legible and do not require that the reader squint to see them. Lastly, have your business cards professionally printed. Whether you design your own online or use a local printer, avoid the temptation of printing your own at home on perforated paper. No matter how fabulous your card looks, it will not leave the impression you want if the tear-away is left poking the recipient.

Address Book

It is important to keep your contact list with you at all times. Whether you carry an address book or keep all your contacts in your phone, you cannot be a go-giver who connects people with other key people in your network if you don't have their information on hand. Try to avoid saying, "I will send you her information later," if you can. You might forget.

Or, you might want to send your new network contact something special at their office. Have a professional way of getting their company name and mailing address upon your meeting. You will leave a far greater impression if you are ready to take down or give out information on the spot. You are more likely to follow up and follow through, too, than if you have to hunt for the right contact information.

Calendar

If you want to make a meeting with someone, have your calendar or planner on hand. You leave a bad impression when you request a meeting with someone but don't know your availability. If your calendar is electronic, you probably always have it with you so you can make spontaneous arrangements to meet someone you have just been introduced to for coffee.

If you prefer a paper calendar, you probably won't carry your datebook or planner to every networking event or dinner party. In a lot of formal situations, not having your calendar is not going to be a big deal. You can arrange to call new connections during working hours, when you are likely to be at your desk and thus will have your calendar in front of you. If you do arrange to call on the person and schedule a face-to-face meeting, having a small paper calendar in your pocket or purse will make you look very organized and will ensure you don't forget to act on your promise to follow up.

The important things is that when you make the call or extend the request, know your schedule and have an answer ready to the question, "Sure, we can meet. What day is good for you?"

Crafting Your Own Sound Bite

It is important that you know exactly what to say when someone asks, "What do you do?" This is where your sound bite comes in handy. Don't just toss out your job title.

Your 10- to 15-second sound bite should explain who you are, what you do, and why you make a difference. You need to do this in a seamless way that sounds very natural.

You need to be able to say…

A) I AM…
B) MY EXPERTISE IS…
C) WHAT I'VE ACHIEVED IS…

For example, my sound bite is:

A) I AM…an editorial producer for CNN.
B) MY EXPERTISE IS…I am a lateral thinker, with tremendous initiative and foresight.
C) WHAT I'VE ACHIEVED IS…the ability to deal with breaking news under very tight time pressures. For example, when Muhammad Ali died I had Evander Holyfield, Don King, and Manny Pacquiao on air within minutes.

Make It Conversational

You are probably aware that written and spoken language are very different, and it is very easy to tell when a politician is reading a speech off a teleprompter. Once you have developed your sound bite, it is important to craft it so that it sounds conversational. The way to do this is to break your sentences down. You may even make some grammatical errors, because spoken English often has incomplete sentences.

So, if someone asks, "What do you do," I might say, "I work at CNN as an editorial producer. Remember the Indian Ocean tsunami in December 2004? I was on call that day, and booked five guests before I even had my first cup of coffee!"

Michelle Watson, the CEO and founder of Topflight Communication, Inc., says the following when asked what she does.

    A) I AM...a book doctor who acts as a personal editorial assistant to self-publishing authors.

    B) MY EXPERTISE IS...crafting non-fiction books and biographies that engage readers.

    C) WHAT I'VE ACHIEVED IS...helping an 80-year-old client fulfill his dreams of becoming a published author by putting out five of his books in one year.

Exercise: *Create Your Fabulous Sound Bite*

Step 1: Develop your own fabulous sound bite by completing the following:

- I AM ...

_____

_____

- MY EXPERTISE IS...

_____

_____

- WHAT I'VE ACHIEVED IS ...

_____

_____

Step 2: Refine and revise. Look to your Positive Emotional Memory Disc for inspiration. Then turn your sound bite into conversational form by cutting down the length of your sentences, and even using one or two incomplete sentences. Practice your sound bite as necessary until it is second nature to you and it just rolls off your tongue—almost without having to think about it. This will have you amply prepared whenever someone important to you pops the question, "And what do you do?"

_____

_____

_____

_____

CHAPTER 12

Follow-Up, Key to Collaboration

Without follow-up, that great connection, great conversation, and great potential will be a great waste!

—Nadia Bilchik, Author and Speaker

Professional practitioners of the art of networking emphasize that *follow-up* is the most important element. "Eighty percent of networking is following up," says Rich Frishman co-author with Jill Lublin of *Networking Magic*. "Don't let relationships languish until you need something," he says. "That's mooching, not networking."

You may recall my comment that fear, more often than time, is what stops most people from networking. Still, I do recognize that many of us have to deal with a time crunch. Nevertheless, responding to someone's e-mail, sending someone an article of interest, inquiring about someone's health, or following up on finding a telephone number for someone, does not take up a lot of time. Also, you can be strategic about follow-up. Once you have invested time in expanding your social network, methodically map out the most important individuals for you to invest in further.

If you truly accept the importance of networking for your professional and personal future, you will set aside the time. One professional I know blocks out about four hours a week on her calendar to spend adding people to her database, updating entries, and sending e-mail. She also attends at least one event a week. Another individual who works in public relations, the ultimate networking job, sets aside a day twice a year to update and reorganize his database of 5,000 names.

In life we find time for what we think of as important. Once you see that networking to build mutually beneficial relationships is a survival tool, you will make it a point to truly set aside the time. Habit is the best survival tool we have in dealing with change; it is our most precious safety net. The goal here is to make network follow-up an automatic part of your life, and not to see this as a separate time-consuming event.

Follow-Up Made Easy

Social networks, if they are used properly, can help you make very efficient use of your time.

In the age of virtual communication, follow-up has never been easier or quicker. Social media networks and e-mail, if they are used properly, can help you make very efficient use of your time. No longer do you have to write a thank you note, find a stamp, and make sure you pass a post office. It is now as easy as a couple of clicks.

I would suggest you follow up within 24 hours of a meeting by taking advantage of e-mail. A simple "thank you" to the person you met yesterday telling them about a press club meeting that may be of interest to them or a support group that focuses on an issue they care about is polite, useful, and effective. If you make sure your e-mail is short, personal, gracious, and specific, you cannot go wrong. The other good news is that, if for any reason they don't reply, you are not dealing with rejection face-to-face.

Being connected all the time does not constitute meaningful social networking.

Expert networkers use all of the communication media at their disposal, but they are careful to do so in a savvy way. Social networking is not about including a potential business contact in your personal "Friends" list, or forwarding those terminally long, "cute" e-mail attachments, or the endless jokes that are always making the rounds. These kinds of messages tend to be irritating, and only in very rare cases do they serve as good follow-up.

In addition, be careful with how you use your e-mail list. If you are sending out a friendly e-mail to a group, make a point of hiding the fact by choosing the "blind copy" option. That way, all of the group's e-mail addresses will not appear. Otherwise, it will look thoughtless to a relative stranger to see a long list of e-mail addresses at the top of the message.

Always put the action or topic of your e-mail in the subject line so the recipient will know it is not spam. And, be sure you personalize your message. People are dealing with electronic overload, so be specific, be conscious of their time, and always check for spelling errors before you hit "Send." Using technology wisely to follow up with someone is an easy way to build rapport.

I have found sending articles or information I think could be of interest to a particular person to be very beneficial in creating rapport. For example, I recently sent a human resources article on the future of supply chain to Soumen Ghosh, the professor of Operations and Supply Chain Management at Georgia Tech. This resulted in a wonderful conversation and a meeting over coffee.

Telling a new contact about a good restaurant you just found, a great book you recently read, or a movie you recommend, are all good examples of helpful follow-up. Bonne Nardi studied successful networkers who have truly adapted to their new, less-structured work environment. She found that to keep their network engines revved, workers constantly attend to three tasks:

- Building a network
- Adding new people to it
- Maintaining it

Of the three, Nardi found that maintenance was the most important task. According to her, "Networking is an ongoing process of keeping a personal network in good repair. In the words of one study participant, 'relationships are managed and fed over time, much as plants are.'"

The people Nardi interviewed emphasized the importance of keeping contacts happy and feeling taken care of. They emphasized that small, personal touches, such as taking people to the most fashionable restaurant, or playing a round of golf with them, yielded out-of-proportion rewards.

The Essentials of Network Maintenance

True networking professionals can be very systematic about the essential task of network maintenance. Nardi cites the example of one individual who is a public relations executive for a large telecommunications company. It is certainly instructive to observe how he goes about "feeding and maintaining" his network.

> You manage it. It really is a planned program of activities. It's a variety of different communications and different forms over time, from calling, sending a fax, something to read, arranging a meeting with the person who is the senior executive. It's offering a theater ticket, inviting someone to a seminar, sending an advance copy of a particular report, and when you have a major announcement, calling them first. Remembering their wife's or their husband's name, understanding what their hobbies are. If one of these people builds canoes and you come across an article about canoe building, you send it to them. In many different ways, it's demonstrating an understanding of who they are and what they're interested in.

Vlad Bog, head of Human Resources for the Coca-Cola Company in Romania, is equally systematic. At a recent networking for success seminar in Bucharest, he described how he goes about network maintenance. He has divided his network into several different categories:

- Close family
- Skiing buddies
- Colleagues
- Coca-Cola bottlers
- Agencies
- Parents of his children's friends
- Old school friends

- Golf buddies
- Former colleagues
- U.S. colleagues

Bog then prioritizes which people in each group require regular contact. Let's call this our "primary network," the people who have earned more of our energy and time. He then very consciously decides on the type of communication he is going to use to maintain the relationship. For example, to stay in touch with certain ski buddies, Bog will send a recent article on special skiing deals that he may have come across in a magazine or newspaper. For business contacts in the bottlers category, he may e-mail weekly updates on sales, or new trends in the bottling industry.

The key to this technique is to be very specific in what you send. Then, people will see that you have taken the time, without being asked, to take their special interests into account.

Dedicated *expert networkers* keep files about their contacts' birthdays, favorite candies or drinks, or any tidbit that may be used to deliver a personalized gift or message. One individual even takes along her list of top 20 contacts when she travels and sends them postcards. Another writes personal letters to his contacts several times a year, trying to pick holidays like Thanksgiving, when his notes won't be lost in a pile of mail.

In one very high-tech solution, someone I know has developed a computer database that beeps after specified intervals to alert him to the fact that he has not called a contact in the database. Facebook's feature that alerts users to upcoming birthdays can also be helpful in providing a reason for outreach and personal interaction.

Expert networkers are also very clear that there is such a thing as too much communication with your network. Only communicate when you have something of value to offer, or when you have something genuine to share. Don't just spam out "Hello, how are you?" notes.

A study from the productivity software firm Boomerang recently found that "thankful closings" in emails received the most positive responses—especially using the cheery, optimistic phrase, "Thanks in advance." Try tweaking your emails to include these types of phrases, rather than the generic "Best" or "Regards" in your closings.

Remember, it is important to follow up in a non-threatening way, and always be sure to say "thank you." Also, don't make the "911 call" to somebody you haven't been in regular contact with. It creates too much pressure. Save these types of requests for people you've kept in touch with and with whom you already have a mutually beneficial relationship.

Exercise: *Maintaining Your Networking Relationships*

Step 1: Think carefully about all the people in your life—both at work and those you know socially. Categorize them into at least six groups (more, if you wish) and enter their names below:

Group 1 CATEGORY:____/ NAMES:

_____

_____

Group 2 CATEGORY:____/ NAMES:

_____

_____

Group 3 CATEGORY:____/ NAMES:

_____

_____

Group 4 CATEGORY:____/ NAMES:

_____

_____

Group 5 CATEGORY:____/ NAMES:

_____

_____

Group 6 CATEGORY:____/ NAMES:

_____

_____

Step 2: Reread the names you wrote and circle the "primary" people in each group.

Step 3: Brainstorm with a friend or colleague on the different ways you could stay in touch with the people on your list. It may be something extravagant like sending football tickets with prime seating to a key client. Or, it could be as simple as an emailed birthday acknowledgement. But, whatever you do, do it with a sense of creativity and originality. Write your ideas for follow-up below.

_____

_____

_____

_____

How to Follow up with Non-Reciprocators

There are cases where some individuals become disenchanted with the whole process. For example, one of my friends complained, "I invest and invest and invest. I give and I'm kind, and it never comes back."

One part of the answer is patience. It might take a year, and it will most likely take a lot longer than you expect. But there is also nothing wrong with reminding certain individuals of the favor you performed—as long as you do it tactfully. You could say, "I'm so pleased I was able to help you on that project; you've done so well. I've got an issue now, and I was wondering how you'd suggest I proceed."

Sometimes people just aren't conscious. We tend to think people are psychic. We like to think they know they should do the right thing. But

sometimes you actually have to

ask. You won't be pushy if you ask in the right way and phrase it correctly. When you ask somebody for assistance, give them options. For example: "Cliff, you have been very successful in the publishing industry. Would you be able to give me a few suggestions on how to get started?"

Just as long as it does not seem that the other party feels they are "entitled," you will find that most people truly enjoy helping others.

CHAPTER 13

Becoming a Networking "Go-To" Person

If someone listens or stretches out a hand, or whispers a kind word of encouragement, or attempts to understand another person, extraordinary things can start to happen.

—Loretta Girzartis, Author

How would you like to become widely recognized as an *expert networker*? Here's the trick: Do not just make the suggestion of introducing two people to each other who could benefit from a meeting, actually go ahead and set up the meeting.

This is how you become what motivational speaker Zig Ziglar described as a "networking go-to person." Networking experts Robert Littell and Donna Fisher describe it as "netweaving." In any case, you are practicing an altruistic "win- win" form of networking in which you concentrate on WIFY (What's in it for you?) rather than WIFM (What's in it for me?). According to Littell, one of the developers of the pay it forward concept, netweaving works in accordance with the golden rule of doing for others as you would want them to do for you, but the assumption, as in the golden rule, is that being generous will have its own rewards.

A Go-To Person in Action

Debra's Story: *Several months ago, I received an email from a woman, Jessica, referring in the subject line to a young fashion designer I'd interviewed a couple years earlier. Jessica, a special projects editor at a national teen magazine, was writing* *to me upon the suggestion of our mutual friend to let me know about her upcoming book, a collection of Latin-inspired entertaining tips and recipes. I corresponded with Jessica over email, then passed along her book information to the appropriate editor, and our magazine ended up doing a small feature on the book.*

Fast forward a few months, and I get a call to do an appearance on ABC's The View. *Accompanying me on the trip was a colleague, Madeleine, who is an art director and was helping to style the segment. Madeleine and I often bounced career ideas off one another, and she mentioned that while in New York for* The View *appearance she would try to do some informational interviewing; she was considering moving to New York to work at a national magazine. I offered to email Jessica—whom I had never met, really barely knew, and had emailed with just a few times—on the off chance that she might be willing to hook Madeleine up to meet with some art directors at her magazine. Jessica agreed wholeheartedly.*

It turns out, Madeleine and Jessica had gone to the same high school in Atlanta, just several years apart! When Madeleine arrived at the magazine, Jessica greeted her with open arms and ushered her into meetings with the magazine's creative director and other senior art directors. After looking at Madeleine's portfolio, the creative director warmly provided her with a list of names of the other magazines that should see her.

This set off a series of excellent informational and job interviews for Madeleine. She just recently accepted a fabulous senior art director position with a top fashion magazine. Who knew my one little email to someone I'd never met could open such doors for a friend of mine?

When you set out to become a networking go-to person for other people, you need to answer two key questions.

How can I put OTHER people together into win- win relationships? The giver does this without expecting anything in return, but has the confidence that benevolence of this kind is often rewarded later on, and often in unexpectedly wonderful ways.

How can I act as a "resource provider" for someone else? This is accomplished either by serving in that role yourself, or by offering others access to your extended network of contacts, including people and information.

The benefit is that you become a strategic resource, which is a powerful position to be in. Instead of being the person in need, you're the person in charge. You're the arranger. It's like becoming a matchmaker, or the hostess, as I described previously in chapter 3.

When someone at CNN asks me for the number of the Sri Lankan Ambassador, I may not know it offhand, but I make the effort to find it. I know with certainty that I will be calling that very same person at some point for assistance, and if I have followed up, the chances of their assisting me go up incrementally.

How do you become this kind of three-dimensional person, who is known by name as a strategic resource—the person recognized as a generous individual who has invested in his network or organization?

- Try to meet face-to-face when possible.
- Most people are receptive, but you should always confirm that they are. (Do not push if you notice reluctance.)
- Never make assumptions; get all the facts before moving ahead. (Feel the person out and ask qualifying questions.)
- Find common ground by discovering what their personal interests are.
- Humanize the person and the conversation. (Do not be judgmental; try to see the world from their viewpoint.)
- Create value by first making the mental connections and then following through. (Send an e-mail that relates to their personal interests.)

"Many managers equate having a good network with having a large database of contacts, or attending high-profile, professional conferences and events," says Herminia Ibarra, a professor of Organizational Behavior at the London Business School.

In fact, we've seen people kick off a networking initiative by improving their record keeping or adopting a network management tool. But they falter at the next step—picking up the phone. Instead, they wait until they need something badly. The best networkers do exactly the opposite: They take every opportunity to give to, and receive from, the network, whether they need help or not.

A network lives and thrives only when it is used. A good way to begin is to make a simple request or take the initiative to connect two people who would benefit from meeting each other. Doing something—anything—gets the ball rolling and builds confidence that one does, in fact, have something to contribute.

You don't need a network so large you can't follow up or serve the people you are connected with. Pick one or two people and build your rapport with them. You network will naturally grow when you are natural.

- Focus on exuding positive energy.
- Have an open, friendly, giving attitude.
- Create opportunities to connect and take advantage of them.
- Make sure your networking is mutually beneficial.
- Actively participate in a forum of your choice.
- Most importantly, follow up with ease and sincerity.

The following is a valuable exercise, so even if you do not have a real-life scenario, make one up. You'll find that even if you have nothing to offer immediately, the opportunities will eventually present themselves. The important thing is that you have set out with the intention of becoming a go-to networker. Also make sure that once you have found what works for you, you *always* follow-up. It sounds easy, but it is the one part of networking where most people slip up.

Exercise: *Being a Networking Go-to Person*

Step 1: Think of a friend or a co-worker you know relatively well. List what you know of their work, their hobbies, and their interests.

_____

_____

Step 2: Make mental connections on where you have common ground, and come up with suggestions of any resources or guidance you can offer.

_____

_____

Step 3: Contact that person via phone or email with your suggestion. Now, expand this exercise out to other people in your network.

In some cases, you may not have anything to offer. That's fine. An *expert networker* knows when to be helpful, but also knows when to pull back. If this is a person you would like to make a connection with at another point, you can be helpful in a subtler way. For example, The parent of one of my daughter's friends is the director of a downtown theater. While I was downtown running personal errands one day, I came across a particularly inviting and pleasant bistro. Later that day, I sent a brief, friendly, and very well-received email telling her about my "find." I am now identified by this theater director as the "go-to" person for fabulous food.

_____

_____

NETWORKING

I am living proof that *expert networking* works, that building mutually beneficial relationships is one of the *best* ways to survive and thrive both personally and professionally. Therefore, I strongly urge you to get started *now*.

NETWORKING can be broken down into the following acronym.

N   be **Natural**
E   be **Enthusiastic**
T   be **Tenacious**
W   **Win** everyone over with your positive attitude
O   see **Opportunity** in every situation
R   be **Relaxed**
K   share your **Knowledge** with others
I   be genuinely **Interested** in others
N   take **No** one for granted
G   be **Generous** and **Giving**

Expert Networking as a Lifestyle

My friend Ney was integral to my family's settling in Atlanta when we first arrived. You can tell from her story that I was just one of the many people whose life she touched, and whom she let touch hers. She built her life around networking in the right ways and for the right reasons.

> **Ney's Story:** *If "necessity is the mother of invention," then "using every trick in the book" is its daughter! Or so I have come to believe as I review the obstacles and "ladders" I have used to achieve the contented and fulfilled life I now lead. Paramount among my "ladders" has been the application of what is today called "networking." Mine has been an unlikely sojourn through contemporary American life, both public and private. It is my collection of people—who, through their presence in my daily life to varying degrees and intensity—have made the trip*

a remarkable adventure in the destinations to which I have arrived and continue to anticipate.

Leaving a small, rural Northern Virginia hamlet populated with a family and a community steeped in the mores and conventions of post-war, mid-century attitudes, I headed for the big city of Philadelphia to seek an education and a future. My first network of friends was as wide and varied as the distance in space and culture I had just traveled.

I first lived in a hostel for young ladies run by Dominican nuns. Little did I know that within the corridors of the Lucy Eaton Smith Residence for Young Ladies was as wild and radical a group of women as I was ever to encounter. Women of all ages, from all parts of the world had come to reside with the Sisters. All, like myself, were seeking to prepare for the next stage of their lives. I found myself exposed to girls whose rooms served as grand salons of music, poetry, and the arts, or were simple holes in the wall for some girl or woman hiding from abuse, adultery, or abortion.

For three years I used my room as a base from which to foray out into various areas of the city, my destination determined only by the fellow resident who accompanied and exposed or guided me. They showed me how to ride a bus, take a taxi, or jump a turnstile. Through them I learned to eat sushi, tamales, borscht, pierogis, and even what it meant to keep Kosher.

During the next 40 years, as I traveled, worked, and lived all over this country, I have sought to duplicate the complexity and diversity of that network of friends. I remained open to all who crossed my path. And, whether it was a big city or a small town, I have eagerly introduced myself to the neighbors, garbage man, postman, and dry cleaner, as well as arriving at my new home with letters of introduction to the most elite of its inhabitants. I have never felt alone or out of place. I have celebrated almost every holiday known to man, and have been embraced and remembered in the prayers of people of every possible religious persuasion. Although never married, I am a special aunt or god-mother to children of all races and creeds, and have an extended family member of every tribe of nationality that inhabits this great melting pot.

I have long espoused the benefits of being open to the treasures available from the most unlikely hands and the affection and joy to be found in relationships with those who, on first glance, appear to be so different from myself. I have found networking to be most rewarding when utilized as a lifestyle rather than a technique. And I have found it to be most effective when one participates, not trying to identify what is "on offer," from the other but confident in the realization that all others offer us new sets of relationships and encounters, each possessing riches of information or experiences.

As I've noted throughout this book, networking has become my passion. Applying the lessons to my own life has enabled me to make an extremely successful transition from one country to another. It has also allowed me to vastly expand my career horizons, and, most importantly, to make meaningful and generous connections with a vast array of wonderful people. If you have read this book closely and mindfully followed the exercises, you too will be in the position to become a generous, engaged, and successful *expert networker* with powerful skills that will enhance all aspects of your life.

I know you can do it.

BIBLIOGRAPHY

Allessandro, Tony. 2000. *Charisma: Seven Keys to Developing the Magnetism that Leads to Success*. New York: Warner Books, Inc.

Brown, S.I.; R.M., A. D. Vinokur, and D. M. Smith. 2003. "Providing Social Support May be More Beneficial than Receiving It: Results from a prospective study of Mortality." *Psychological Science* 14 (4): 320-27.

Canfield, Jack, Mark Victor Hansen, Martin I. Ruttel, Maida Rogerson. 2001. *Chicken Soup for the Soul at Work*. Deerfield Beach: Health Communications, Inc.

Chopra, Deepak. 1995. *Seven Spiritual Laws of Success: A Practical Guide to the Fulfillment of your Dreams*. San Rafael: Amber-Allen Publishing.

Eisenberger, N.I. and M. D. Lieberman. 2004. "Why Rejection Hurts: A Common Neural Alarm System for Physical and Social Pain." *Trends in Cognitive Sciences*, I: 294-300.

Eng, Patricia M.; Eric B. Rimmi, Garrett Fitzmaurice, and Ichiro Kawachi. 2002. "Social Ties and Change in Relation to Subsequent Total and Cause-Specific mortality and Coronary Heart Disease Incidence n Men." *American Journal of Epidemiology*, 155 (8): 700-09.

Erickson, Bonnie. 2003. "Social Networks: The Value of Variety." *Contexts: Understanding People in their Social Worlds*, 2 (1) Retrieved from: HTTP:// www.contextsmagazine.org/content_sample_v2- 1.php.

Ferrazzi, Keith; and Tahl Raz. 2005. *Never Eat Alone: And Other Secrets to Success, One Relationship at a Time*. New York: Doubleday Publishing.

Frishman, Rick, Jill Lublin, Jill, and Mark Steisel. 2004. *Networking Magic: Find the Best—From Doctors, Lawyers, and Accounts, to Homes, Schools and Jobs*. New York: Adams Media Corporation.

Futch, Ken. 2005. *Take Your Best Shot: Turning Situations into Opportunities*. Atlanta: Wagrub Press.

Goleman, Daniel. 2005. *Working with Emotional Intelligence*. New York: Bantam Books.

Granovetter, M.S. 1973. "The Strength of Weak Ties." *American Journal of Sociology*, 6: 1360-80

Hansen, Kristin A. 2001. "Geographical Mobility." *US Census Bureau*. January 18. Retrieved from: http://www.census.gov.

Healy, Melissa. 2005. "Girlfriends: They May Promote Health." *The Los Angeles Times*, May 26.

Ihrke, David. 2014. "Reason for Moving." June. Retrieved July 23, 2018 from https://www.census.gov/content/dam/Census/library/publications/2014/demo/p20-574.pdf

Kehoe, John.1997. *Mind Power into the 21ˢᵗ Century. Techniques for Success and Happiness.* Vancouver: Zoetic Books.

Klaus, Peggy. 2004. *Brag!: The Art of Tooting Your Own Horn Without Blowing It.* New York: Warner Business.

Lin, Nan. 2001. "Building a Theory of Social Capital." *Social Capital: Theory and Research.* New York: Routledge: 3-30.

Little, Robert S. and Donna Fisher. 2001. *Power Netweaving: 10 Secrets to Successful Relationship Marketing.* Erlanger: National Underwriting Company.

Mackay, Harve B. 2005. *Swim with the Sharks Without Being Eaten Alive.* New York: HarperCollins Publishers.

Nardi, Bonnie A, Steve Whittaker, and Heinrich Schwarz. 2000. "It's Not What You Know, It's Who You Know: Work in the Information Age." *First Monday: A Peer- Reviewed Journal on the Internet.* Retrieved from: http://www.firstmonday.org/issues/issues_5/nardi/

Roane, Susan. 2000. *How to Work a Room: The Ultimate Guide to Savvy Socializing in Person and Online.* New York: HarperCollins Publishers.

Robbins, Anthony. 1992. *Awaken the Giant Within: How to Take Immediate Control of Your Mental, Emotional, Physical and Financial Destiny.* New York: Simon and Schuster Adult Publishing Group.

Robbins, Anthony, Joseph McClendon, and Dominick V. Anfuso. 2006. *Inner Strength: Harnessing the Power of Your Six Primal Needs.* New York: The Free Press.

Ruiz, Don Miguel (1997). *The Four Agreements.* San Rafael: Amber-Allen Publishing.

Rutledge, Thomas; Steven E. Reis, Marian Olson, James Owens, Shertl F. Kelsey, Carl J. Pepine, Sunii Manka, William J. Rogers, C. Noel Bairey Merz, George Sopko, Carol E. Cornell, Barry Sharaf, and Karen A. Matthews. 2004. "Social Networks are associated with Lower Mortality Rates Among Women with Suspected Coronary Disease: The National Heart, Lung, and Blood Institute-Sponsored Women's Ischeia Syndrome Evaluation Study." *Psychosomatic Medicine,* 66: 882-88.

Siebert, Scott E.; Maria L. Kraimer, and Robert C. Liden. 2001. A Social Capital Theory of Career Success. *Academy of Management Journal.*

Silk, Joan B.; Susan C. Alberts, and Jeanne Altmann. 2003. "Social Bonds of Female Baboons Enhance Infant Survival." *Science* 302, 5648: 1231-34.

Swanbrown, Diane. 1998. "To Retire Well, Invest in Making Friends." *EurekaAlert!* Retrieved from: http://www.eurekealert.org.

U.S. Census Bureau Report. *Geographical Mobility: 2012 to 2013*, released November 18, 2013.

Ziglar, Zig. 2000. *See You At The Top.* Gretna: Pelican Publishing Company, Inc.

TO BOOK NADIA

Nadia is available to speak through

Greater Impact Communication

TRAINING TOPICS INCLUDE:

Maximizing Your Presentation Impact

Presentation skill training to ensure participants are H.E.A.R.D. and that they maximize every presentation opportunity.

Professional/Executive/Leadership Presence

Participants learn tips and techniques, and develop a mindset to project the best version of themselves and understand that everything they do and say communicates.

Brand YOU: Maximize Your Presence & Leverage the Power of Your Personal Brand

Participants learn, develop, communicate, and leverage their unique strengths in a way that benefits both the individual and the business.

What's Your Style?

Learn how your personality impacts your communication.

Bridging Communication Gaps

Learn how to communicate with clarity and confidence in a high-stakes business environment.

Networking for Success

Participants develop techniques and the mindset needed to build value-based and inclusive relationships in a diverse business environment.

Nadia's Keynote Topics Include:

- Unleashing the Power of Your Personal Presence
- Lighting the FIRE: Build Rapport EVERY Time You Communicate
- Kick Your Relationships up a Notch
- Brand You
- Own Your Space: The Woman's Guide to Polish, Poise, and Empowerment

For more information on these and other programs contact:
www.nadiabilchik.com | steve@nadiabilchik.com
404-274-4367

CPSIA information can be obtained
at www.ICGtesting.com
Printed in the USA
BVHW062354261221
624770BV00007B/532